W9-BMT-561

EMOTIONAL
SUCCESS

EMOTIONAL SUCCESS

THE POWER OF GRATITUDE, COMPASSION, AND PRIDE

DAVID DeSTENO

An Eamon Dolan Book
Houghton Mifflin Harcourt
Boston New York
2018

For information about permission to reproduce selections from this book,
write to trade.permissions@hmhco.com or to Permissions,
Houghton Mifflin Harcourt Publishing Company,
3 Park Avenue, 19th Floor, New York, New York 10016.

hmhco.com

Library of Congress Cataloging-in-Publication Data is available.
ISBN 978-0-544-70310-0

Book design by Greta D. Sibley

Printed in the United States of America
DOC 10 9 8 7 6 5 4 3 2 1

To my family

CONTENTS

INTRODUCTION

Self-Control, Success, and the Road Not Taken

Me want cookie... but me wait. For almost anyone who was or lived with a child sometime in the past forty years, the first part of that sentence calls up images of a blue, fuzzy, grammatically challenged, adorably gluttonous Muppet: Cookie Monster. But the second part caught me off guard when I first heard it. Cookie, as his name implies, was traditionally an embodiment of immediate gratification. Sure, once in a while he was tweaked to accommodate the concerns of the time. When the healthiness of kids' diets was in question, Cookie's penchant for sweets was changed to include fruit. When the dangers of food allergies in schools became apparent, he made sure his cookies were nut-free. Yet across the years, one trait remained constant: impulsivity. When Cookie wanted something, he wanted it *now*. But in 2013, during *Sesame Street*'s forty-fourth season, that changed; *but me wait* became part of Cookie's Muppet mantra and, as a result, part of a new generation's early education.

This change is evidence of our society's continuing obsession with success. And when it comes to achieving that success, whether it's at the office, in managing finances, in bettering health, or even in pursuing an unlikely dream, decades of research has revealed that self-control is key. By that, I mean the ability to resist urges for immediate gratification in order to obtain greater rewards in the future.

Best-selling books such as *Willpower, How Children Succeed,* and *Grit* all promise insight into how perseverance and patience can affect our lives for the better. Not to be outdone, magazines from the *Atlantic* to *People* routinely feature articles on the benefits of self-control and how to obtain it.

I don't mean to criticize this emphasis on self-control and valuing the future. To the contrary, I think we need it. And while the idea of self-control's benefits isn't new — we can see it extolled in moral tales and treatises going back for centuries — what is new is that this idea has moved from philosophy and theology into empirical proof. The benefits of self-control aren't a matter of opinion anymore; they're quantifiable. And what can be quantified can, in theory, be maximized. The million-dollar question, of course, is *How?* How can self-control be enhanced?

It's here that I fear we have gone astray. For almost fifty years we've been developing science-based strategies meant to help us reach our goals. Yet on average, we are no better at delaying immediate gratification than we were in the 1960s. If anything, our impatience and desire for immediate satisfaction are on the rise. As individuals and as a society, we're spending more on impulse buys and conveniences rather than saving for a rainy day or retirement. We're diverting our attention to games or social media on our smartphones rather than focusing it on learning and honing skills we need. We're satisfying our sweet tooth and, as a result, expanding our waists simply to gain momentary pleasures at a great cost to our future well-being. And at a more macro level, many of us are resisting choices such as spending a bit more for clean or renewable energy that, though somewhat costlier in the moment, will help avoid greater problems down the road. In short, we're planning less for the future, not caring as much about what that future will bring. And while it's undoubtedly true that each of these examples of impatience and shortsightedness stems from many factors, underlying them all is a growing bias toward pleasure in the moment.

On any given day, most people fail to stick with their daily goals about 20 percent of the time — a percentage that climbs quickly if they're busy, tired, or stressed. That means almost one out of every five times we try to work harder, eat better, save more, or prepare for a test or performance evaluation, we're going to fail to do it in favor of something else that's more fun in the moment. And when decisions involve important goals — the ones that truly matter to people — the success rate is even worse. Only 8 percent of New Year's resolutions are kept throughout the year. While 25 percent fail in the first week. The result is that most of us frequently end up feeling powerless to stick to our goals and, even worse, upset with ourselves for loafing, splurging, bingeing, or otherwise giving in to a desire for some short-term pleasure that will ultimately cost us.

This raises an intriguing and troubling question: If delaying gratification and valuing the future are so important, and if we've been using science-backed strategies for decades to help us do it, why are most of us still so bad at it? One would think that our minds would come equipped with tools to meet the challenges posed by a lack of impulse control. After all, that's one hallmark of evolutionary development: the mind and body retain features that help us to thrive. So, either the development of the human mind has a gaping hole, as the need for self-control has been around since our species's beginning, or we're doing something wrong. And as a scientist who for decades has studied how humans make decisions, I can confirm that it's the latter.

Our minds do come equipped with the necessary tools to succeed, but we're forsaking them. We still have serious problems delaying gratification, developing dedication, and cultivating perseverance because our notion of how self-control works is flawed. Put simply, we're seeing only half the picture. When we're forced to choose strategies for success, we tend to favor cognitive ones — stoic approaches characterized by reason, deliberation, and force of will. If you read those bestsellers I mentioned, page through popular magazines, or even peruse scientific papers, you'll find the same underlying message: rationality trumps emotion. To stand firm in the face of challenges and temptations, we're told to use what psychologists term *executive function* — that part of the mind that manages and controls "subordinate" processes such as memory, attention, and feelings. The term *executive* wasn't picked by accident. This aspect of the mind is, in essence, the boss; it gives the orders that the rest of the mind is supposed to follow. Executive function allows people to plan, to reason, and to use willpower to keep focused, accept sacrifices, and ignore or suppress emotional responses that might get in the way of reaching their long-term aspirations. And cognitive strategies such as these — ones based on reason and analysis as opposed to emotions — are believed to maintain the perseverance required to succeed.

But the fact that a given set of tools sometimes works doesn't imply that it will always work. Nor does it imply that they're the best tools for the job. In the case of our reliance on cognitive tools such as willpower, I believe we've created a predicament. We've ended up with a set of tools that, while effective at times, is inefficient and fragile. More troubling, under certain circumstances these tools can even be harmful. The upshot of using them is that we're often setting ourselves up for failure while increasing the likelihood of damage to our physical and mental well-being over the long run.

THE FALSE CHOICE

For centuries philosophers, psychologists, and people in general pitted cognition — those supposedly rational, logical mechanisms of the mind that feel like you can guide them — against emotion — those supposedly irrational and capricious components that seem to emerge unbidden — when trying to understand how we make decisions. And for most of that time we've tended to trumpet the former while stigmatizing the latter.

This one-to-one mapping of reason to virtue and emotion to vice doesn't reflect reality, however. It sets up a false choice. As we'll see in the chapters that follow, the mind has emotions because, more often than not, they help us. In psychological parlance, they're adaptive. They nudge, or sometimes thrust, our decisions in ways meant to help us achieve our goals, not to thwart them. We often miss this essential truth when we fail to recognize that the decision-making machinery of the human mind is quite complex. It often must manage competing goals, some of which are focused on present outcomes and others on future ones. If it's true — as most researchers in the field believe — that emotions did evolve to be adaptive, then it follows that some must be attuned to short-term needs and wants while others are attuned to costs and benefits coming down the line. Yet when it comes to self-control, almost all studies of emotion have focused on those feelings relevant to the short term — emotions such as anger, lust, and desire, which favor satisfaction of an immediate craving or impulse.

Even among psychologists, the prevailing view of how we should develop self-restraint, diligence, grit, and the like can be boiled down to something quite simple: cognition is good, emotions are bad. Most believe that the best way for people to resist eating the second piece of chocolate cake, spending their paycheck on an impulse buy, or watching a movie when they should be working is for their mental executive to marshal its army of cognitive tools and overcome emotions bent on satisfying cravings for immediate pleasure. As a result, experts and friends tell us to use reason to convince ourselves that saving money or going to the gym is worthwhile. To use techniques such as distraction to keep ourselves or our kids from reaching back into the cookie jar. And, if necessary, to use willpower to make ourselves stick to the plan.

Unfortunately, when these strategies are used too frequently or under demanding conditions, they often fail. For example, each time a person uses willpower and executive function to resist temptations in relatively quick succession, those tools become less effective. Likewise, strategies based on distracting oneself from a short-term desire become more difficult to implement the closer any desired object looms — a perverse fact given that this is when we need self-control most. We're *never* told to use an emotion itself to achieve a challenging goal. This is unfortunate, even tragic, because emotions can be such powerful tools for maintaining self-control. On balance, they're both easier to use and more robust than the cognitive tools we're told to reach for.

Sure, emotions can lead us astray. We've all felt the distracting pull of pleasure when confronting a difficult task. We've felt listless when depressed or eager for a quick fix or guilty pleasure. We've felt angry and wanted to lash out even when we know doing so might be harmful to others and ourselves. Yet we're making a profound mistake if we assume that just because some emotions can lead us into temptation, *all* emotions will. If emotions always guided our decisions in problematic ways, we wouldn't have them; they would have been left in the evolutionary dustbin long ago.

In truth, emotions are among the most powerful and efficient mechanisms we have to guide good decisions. They're the first such mechanisms we developed, too. Emotional responses existed long before we acquired the cognitive abilities to plan ahead — abilities that reside in the frontal lobe of modern humans — yet still faced the challenges posed by short-term desires (for example, to eat all the food rather than share with our fellows). The trick to success, then, comes in understanding that emotions don't only *happen to us; we* can use them to help achieve our goals — if we develop the wisdom to call upon the right emotions to meet the challenges at hand.

When it comes to long-term success, the "right" emotions are principally these: gratitude, compassion, and pride. These emotions, unlike basic feelings of happiness, sadness, anger, or fear, are intrinsically tied to social life, and that provides the key to their effectiveness. At base, social living regularly requires a willingness to accept costs in the moment to ensure better days ahead. We didn't originally develop self-control so that we could study for exams, save for retirement, or go to the gym. For most of our evolutionary history, none of that mattered or even existed. What did matter to survive and thrive was having strong social bonds — relationships that would encourage people to lend support to others in need while knowing full well that their sacrifices would be returned if and when required in the future. Establishing and maintaining such relationships required behaving morally. It meant being fair, being honest, being generous, being diligent, and being loyal. In short, morality itself was adaptive; being perceived to have good character marked a person as capable of overcoming a desire to be overly selfish and, therefore, as a person with whom it was safe to partner. And as we'll see, it's precisely the emotions of gratitude, compassion, and pride that make us more willing to behave in these valued ways.

Think about the last time you felt any of these three states — really felt them. They probably pushed you to accept some type of immediate cost. Gratitude has led me to spend many hours repaying favors or debts. I've moved more couches and spent more time making gifts for friends than I thought possible, all to make sure that others whose friendships I valued knew I appreciated what they had done for me and, in so doing, kept those bonds from fraying down the line. Compassion is similar. It moves many people to give money, time, or emotional support to others in need. It encourages an altruism that ensures efforts will be returned for our kind acts when we need them. Pride, too, can encourage people to sacrifice for future gain. I'll always remember one of my students telling me that the only thing that allowed her to get up at 5:00 a.m. every day to practice rowing on the frigid Columbia River was the pride she felt in being part of her team. These emotions grease the wheels of social life by making us act in ways that, though costly to our pleasure or resources in the short term, bring the promise of greater rewards in the future. They *give* us self-control.

These same emotions — the ones that push us to value the future in order to grow our social success — can be co-opted to help us achieve success in any area of life: academic, professional, financial, health. Just as they nudge us to sacrifice in the short run to better our relationships with others, we can use them to manage our relationships with someone else who's central to our hopes and dreams: our own future selves. As we'll see, cultivating these three emotions can help us meet our own needs and goals in a way that is more powerful and less fraught than relying on reason and willpower alone.

COLLATERAL DAMAGE

Depending on fragile cognitive strategies to reach our goals doesn't only reduce our chances of success, it can also harm us in more subtle ways. Broadly speaking, these harms — what I call collateral damage — tend to be of two types. The first centers on stress. Because most of the cognitive techniques are corrective in nature — they're meant to override or tamp down a more basic desire for pleasure rather than prevent that desire from emerging in the first place — they usually require a good deal of effort. It can frequently feel like you're wrestling with yourself as you pursue a goal. And since few experiences cause more stress than those that combine great effort with a sizable risk of failure, feelings of tension and temporary burnout can arise. This kind of stress isn't only unpleasant, it also has been shown to interfere with our ability to learn. So in some ways, using cognitive techniques is like taking two steps forward and one step back. Over time, however, the negative effects from using these tools can be even more pernicious; they can lead to declines in health.

This brings us to the second form of collateral damage. Although a bit more diffuse, the impairments are no less troubling. In modern life, success for many requires gaining more and more competence in highly specific realms. If you want to be a top violinist, you've got to practice for hours and hours to hone your craft and stay one step ahead of the competition. If you want to get into Harvard Medical School, Yale Law, or a famed Silicon Valley corporation, it's much the same. Competition is fierce, meaning dedication to building knowledge and skills is essential. How we choose to motivate ourselves to do this, however, can make a world of difference.

The currently recommended ways — the ones that rely on executive function, reason, and the like — all share a theme: rational antisocialism. That is, they treat the mind as if it were a machine existing in a social vacuum, with engineers tweaking its mechanisms to make it ever more efficient. If you want to succeed, the thinking goes, work harder, faster, longer, and more efficiently. That's what a computer or robot would do. So, if you're a human, who unlike those entities is saddled with temptations to seek multiple types of enjoyment, do everything you can to suppress those. Bring willpower online to thwart irrational emotional responses that might lead you astray. When willpower fails, use techniques of distraction, habit formation, goal reappraisal, and the like. But the human mind isn't a computer. It has an owner who is a social being, meaning that it evolved to take care of a body that has social needs — needs that these cognitive mechanisms often ignore or even inhibit — that are also inherently linked to achievement. As we'll see later in this book, links to other people not only drive perseverance and success but also make us more fulfilled and resilient.

The personality trait of grit — the ability to use self-control to keep focused on future goals over long periods — has been linked to achievement. This makes great sense, as those who are habitually more willing to accept sacrifices in the short run to enhance their skills in the long run are more likely to reach their goals. But, and it's a big *but,* it's a risky approach.

One of the most celebrated early findings in grit research came from a study of the prestigious pressure cooker that is the Scripps National Spelling Bee. Although on its own, grit was clearly predictive of success — kids who had higher levels of grit were more likely to advance through initial stages — there were some cautionary findings as well. For example, in the final rounds, once differences in verbal IQ and age were considered, differences in grit were virtually meaningless. In other words, a child's level of intelligence combined with experience based on age trumped any influence grit had in determining who won the bee or came close among this select group of finalists. What it did predict among these high achievers was longer hours spent studying and drilling vocabulary words — longer hours that didn't correspond to better performance but did likely increase social isolation. And few factors are more closely associated with unhappiness or poor health than loneliness and social isolation. So while grit is undoubtedly important, the tools and strategies a person uses to become gritty can matter greatly.

More evidence of the threats posed by using a strictly cognitive tool set to keep your nose to the grindstone comes from research done by the psychologist Christopher Boyce and colleagues. Boyce's team followed more than nine thousand people for four years as they faced possible failures such as losing a job. They found that people who were highly self-disciplined in their pursuits and who tended to rely on logical analysis and willpower-related self-control to achieve their goals were also the ones who suffered the most when facing failure. While losing a job is difficult for anyone, the drop in well-being among these people was 120 percent greater than among others. These hardworking people do fail less often, but when they do, it takes a greater toll on them, as they have a weaker safety net to catch them when they fall.

The way out of this trap — the way to improve our chances of achieving while also building resilience — is simply to use the emotional tools available to us. As we'll see, using gratitude, compassion, and pride to pursue our goals will enable us to persevere and resist temptation — to increase our self-control and grit — while almost effortlessly helping us create the social bonds that will buttress us against stumbles, stress, and the afflictions of loneliness along the way.

THE JOURNEY AHEAD

This book will examine the origins and workings of these three emotions, their ties to self-control and resilience, and their potential for increasing success over the long haul for each of us and for society at large. To do this, I've divided the book into three parts. In the first — Setting the Stage — I describe the problem and then dispel our fundamental misconceptions about how to solve it. In chapter 1, I'll briefly review why the human mind prefers short-term rewards over long-term ones, the problems this preference causes, and why almost everyone will succumb to temptation under certain circumstances. Then, in chapter 2, I'll dispel the fallacy that cognition is the only route to self-control by demonstrating the many foibles inherent in relying on reason, willpower, and executive function to get the job done.

In the second part of the book, The Emotional Toolbox, I'll show how gratitude, compassion, and pride, when cultivated and used appropriately, provide the strongest bulwark against the indulgence and impulsivity that often underlie failure. Gratitude and compassion are not passive; they are states of quiet power. Pride, when used properly, is not destructive but rather beneficial as it focuses the mind on the future. As we explore each of these emotions in turn (chapters 3–5), we'll examine not only how and why they shape our behaviors but also ways to use them effectively.

In the book's third and final part — Value Added — I'll explain how adopting emotion-based strategies might offer the most robust way forward both for individuals and for society as a whole. In chapter 6 I'll show how gratitude, compassion, and pride build social relationships — their original purpose — that offer a double benefit. In addition to reinforcing grit and self-control on their own, relationships function to keep loneliness, and all its harms to mind and body, at bay.

In chapter 7 I'll expand the social view by showing how these emotions can flow through a social network, thereby increasing not only your own success but also that of those around you. The bonus here is that you, too, will benefit when others invite these emotions into play. And in chapter 8 I'll extend the field of view once again, this time to the societal level. Here we'll take a look at how using and cultivating these emotions among larger groups of people can help ensure a society's resilience by increasing its willingness to invest in its future.

Finally, in the Coda, I'll reflect on both how this new perspective should change our thinking about the pursuit of success and how strategies using these three emotions should be better implemented. With respect to altering our thinking, it's important to recognize two things. First, from a scientific perspective, gratitude, compassion, and pride aren't just three independent human virtues; they're actually the source of many others. Second, emotions aren't just foisted upon us; we can exert great control over what we feel and when we feel it. In combination, these truths give rise to an entirely new way of understanding how certain emotions can be used to help us thrive. Yet at present too few professionals — whether they be educators, corporate trainers, managers, or counselors — have embraced this view, and thus too few people are equipped with the techniques necessary to pursue their goals most effectively. It's time we change that, because if we're going to meet the challenges our lives and careers throw at us, many of which require patience, dedication, and fortitude to overcome, we're going to need every weapon in our arsenal.

Part 1

SETTING THE STAGE

The Problem

Why and How We All Devalue the Future

One marshmallow now, or two later? It's not the kind of question you'd expect to launch a scientific revolution. But fifty years ago it did just that. At the Bing Nursery School on the campus of Stanford University, psychologist Walter Mischel began a series of experiments that would form the basis for the modern understanding of self-control and, as a result, the ways people pursue their goals. These experiments, which have colloquially come to be known as the marshmallow test, allowed development of a prognostic tool that had been something of a holy grail for behavioral scientists. It offered a way to identify who was most likely to succeed — a sorting ability that would be invaluable to educators, employers, and recruiters alike.

At its heart, the marshmallow test was principally about the ability to resist temptation. It confronted children with a tantalizing, time-dependent dilemma. They could immediately devour the single treat a researcher had placed on the table in front of them (most often a marshmallow, hence the name) or, if they could resist the urge to eat it until the researcher returned from running an errand down the hall, they'd double their prize: they'd get two. Although the choice appears simple enough, it turned out that a given child's success or failure in resisting that first treat didn't reflect just a random choice on a random day. It offered a window into the future — a glimpse of how the child would deal with the many temptations embedded in a life yet to come. The kids who could wait — the ones who could resist the desire for immediate gratification — ended up with much more than two marshmallows in the decades ahead.

As Mischel's team followed the children through the years, a consistent pattern emerged. Those who were better at resisting temptation in preschool prospered in comparison with their more impulsive counterparts. They not only had better grades, but they outperformed the marshmallow gobblers on the SAT by more than two hundred points, thereby upping their chances for admission to selective colleges. Perhaps more surprising was that greater achievement wasn't limited to academic realms. Increased self-control also predicted better social relationships and health. The preschoolers who demonstrated more patience grew into adults who had stronger and more numerous friendships, were less obese, and were less likely to abuse drugs or engage in other addictive behaviors. Likewise, research on other adults — not those from Mischel's initial studies — has shown better self-control to underlie increased financial well-being in the form of better retirement savings and lower levels of debt.

Put simply, the ability to control your impulses matters in life. Whether we're talking about studying, practicing, saving, exercising, or persevering, a willingness to sacrifice in the moment to gain greater rewards in the future can often make all the difference. Yet, as I noted at this book's beginning, it seems a bit odd that an ability that is so closely linked to success often feels so precarious to use. Put another way, if using self-control to resist short-term pleasures has *always* been the best choice, it shouldn't be so hard to master. Evolution should have eased its path. But given that self-control is so often hard to attain and sustain, its tenuousness must represent either a strange glitch or a more complex dynamic than most people realize. To find out which it is, we need to peer into the workings of the mind a bit more closely.

OF ANTS AND GRASSHOPPERS

It's a basic fact of life that we don't feel the *full* effects of many decisions immediately. As with a growing seedling or a festering wound, we often need time to appreciate a decision's results. Sometimes this doesn't pose much of a problem. If both the immediate and future results of a decision are positive, there's no dilemma. If a person loves going to the gym and has ample time to do it, all is good. Exercising not only gives pleasure in the moment but also increases physical fitness, which down the road will itself lead to better health. The difficulty in decision making comes when the costs and benefits of a choice aren't consistent over time. Many choices pose temporal tradeoffs, meaning that the costs or benefits they offer in the moment aren't similar in scope to those that will accrue over time. What you choose to eat, whether and how you choose to invest, how you spend your free time — these decisions often offer starkly different gains or losses as time marches on. Eating that extra order of fries might feel great in the moment but will likely result in a more stressful experience during next week's weight check at the doctor's office. Diverting cash from retirement savings to a lease on a sleek new BMW, while providing a fashionable and enviable ride, will reduce comfort later in life. Even an enjoyable visit to the gym can result in future costs if it comes at the expense of studying for an exam at school or preparing a presentation for work.

These types of situations — where different consequences unfold as time progresses — are known as dilemmas of intertemporal choice. And we face them daily. Every time a person chooses to direct effort or resources toward one activity or goal instead of another, it's highly likely that a tradeoff is involved, whether or not it is consciously considered. The question is how to decide. How should you choose between working diligently for the next few hours on a project or going to the theater to see a movie that interests you? Logic dictates that if a person is focused on maximizing utility — by which economists mean satisfaction — the decision strategy is clear. Compare the utility from watching an enjoyable film with that resulting from a salary bonus or promotion that's likely to come from completing an important project on schedule, and the answer should be simple. In most cases, the long-term gains from the latter will far outweigh the immediate pleasures of the former. Working hard now will provide the opportunity for many more cinematic outings in the years to come — outings that would be more easily purchased because of increased income.

As this example suggests, when it comes to decisions involving effort or expenditure, our minds focus on weighing alternatives. To borrow one of Aesop's most famous motifs, we must decide whether to be an ant or a grasshopper.

For those who don't know or remember the old fable, it describes the joys and travails of two creatures with decidedly different work ethics. At the start of the summer, an ant and a grasshopper have to decide how to spend their time. The industrious ant resists the temptation to play in the warm sun and instead toils away collecting and storing food for the cold months ahead. The blithe grasshopper does just the opposite. He spends the summer singing and dancing, as food is plentiful during the warm months. When the cold of winter finally arrives, the ant is prepared with enough food to see her through. The grasshopper starves after being chastised by the ant for his idle ways.

This tale has long been used to teach children the idea that hard work at the expense of play is often necessary to overcome challenges and ensure prosperity (or at least survival). It also provides a perfect motif for capturing the dynamics involved in self-control. The grasshopper symbolizes the value of immediate pleasure. The ant symbolizes the opposite: the value of future rewards that entail immediate cost. If your mindset favors the grasshopper in one instance, decisions will favor short-term rewards — the temptation to go out to the movies will trump a motivation to work on an important project. Conversely, if it favors the ant, the desire for future rewards in the form of recognition and salary will keep you focused on the task at hand, even though doing so will require some sacrifice now. Whether we're talking about money, food choice, practice, or keeping promises, this same metaphor applies. The mind is always busy estimating the differing values of immediate and future rewards.

All in all, this seems like a reasonable decision framework. As we'll see below, sometimes valuing short-term rewards can make sense. If it didn't, we wouldn't have any such desires in the first place. All we need to make good decisions, then, is an unbiased mental algorithm — one that objectively and accurately determines which "insect" we should emulate in any given instance. Unfortunately, there is no such algorithm. The human mind has a built-in bias toward the present. It tends to want pleasure now and discount the value of future rewards. As a result, for the ant to beat the grasshopper, a future reward would need to substantially outweigh an immediate one. Otherwise, like the grasshopper, we'll choose to eat, dance, procrastinate, and be merry as opposed to work, save, or otherwise diligently lay the groundwork for future success. Whether this is a bug or feature of the brain's "software" depends not on how but on when you ask the question.

BACKWARD DEPRECIATION

To understand why we tend to devalue the future so much, we need to alter the way we typically think about depreciation. Many things we purchase begin to depreciate immediately. Drive a new car off the lot, and it's already worth less. Use a laptop for a few months, and it's lost significant value. But when it comes to intertemporal choice, depreciation works kind of in reverse. The perceived value of objects or rewards you don't yet have decreases as they move further into the future. So, for example, a new car coming right off the assembly line seems worth less if you'll be getting it in six months than in six weeks. This phenomenon — termed *temporal* or *delay discounting* — has long been recognized by economists. To many of them, especially those who dominated twentieth-century economic thought, discounting was a regrettable hiccup of the mind. Devaluing future goods in the absence of any solid reason for doing so seemed illogical to these thinkers, who believed that humans could — or at least should — make only purely rational economic decisions.

Economists' laments aside, temporal discounting is a well-established fact of mental life. Here's an example of how it works. Let's say the government were to offer a tax refund of $100. Most people would happily take it, of course. But now let's say the government offered two options for that refund. You could take the $100 immediately with no strings attached, or you could invest that $100 in a bond for a guaranteed 400 percent return in a year's time. Now what would you do? Believe it or not, most people would still opt to take the $100 now rather than $500 a year from now, even though the latter would be the best investment option most would ever have.

It might seem ludicrous that people would pass up a 400 percent return, but numerous experiments have proven as much. Let me offer some evidence from my own lab. We invited folks from the Greater Boston Area into our facility and placed each person in a separate cubicle with a computer. We informed them that the computer would present twenty-seven questions, one at a time, which would ask them to select which of two monetary options they would prefer. Each question took the form of "Would you rather have $X now, or $Y in Z days?" And to make the stakes real, we told people that we would select one of their choices at random and honor it. If, for instance, we chose the item "Would you rather have $41 dollars now or $75 in twenty days?" for a given person who had indicated a preference for the immediate payout, we'd hand her $41 at the end of the session. If she had indicated a preference for the delayed reward, we'd send her a check for $75 in twenty days.

Now, the values for X, Y, and Z weren't random. Y was always larger than X, as it wouldn't make sense to forgo an immediate reward for a future one that was smaller. By varying the differences between individual pairs of X's and Y's while also changing how long people would have to wait for the delayed reward, we were able to calculate a measure of how much any person devalued future financial rewards. This measure took the form of *an annual discount factor* (ADF), which is a number that ranges between 0 and 1 and reflects the value a fixed amount to be received in one year has relative to the same amount if it were received immediately. In other words, if a person has an ADF of .50, it means he would perceive $100 in a year from now as equivalent in value to $50 today. In other words, an ADF of .50 means that this person would be willing to accept $50 today to forgo getting $100 in a year.

People in our experiment were pretty impatient, as is typical. The average ADF was .17, meaning that the average person perceived $100 to be worth only $17 if he had to wait a year to get it. Put differently, it meant that if I offered this typical person anything more than $17 now to forgo the opportunity to receive $100 in a year, he'd take it in a heartbeat. That's a good deal of financial impatience, as turning $17 into $100 after only a year ends up equaling a return on investment of over 400 percent. Unless a person needed that $17 to survive, physically or metaphorically, for the next few days, this decision makes little sense. It seems excessively shortsighted, as in a year's time the purchasing power would be a lot more.

The question of why this myopia exists in a brain that is supposed to be adaptive is a good one. The answer, however, is a bit convoluted because discounting can make sense under certain conditions. Remember the old adage that a bird in the hand is worth two in the bush? No one would deny, objectively speaking, that two birds would fill your stomach better than one. But when it comes to comparing the certainty of having a single bird versus the uncertainty of bagging two or being left with none, the desirability of the options available to fill a hungry belly becomes a bit dicier. It's the same with dilemmas of intertemporal choice. No one disputes that $100 in a year will be worth more than $17 would be now, but the utility of waiting for that $100 depends heavily on the certainty that the $100 will actually be available for you. What if the bank goes under? What if you go under — six feet under, that is? Sacrifice in the moment has benefits only to the extent that future rewards are guaranteed to flow from it.

Life in an uncertain world requires weighing rewards with an eye toward probability. Perceived values do not, and should not, equal objective values when future rewards aren't set in stone. In many ways, it's like gambling. Who would plunk down fifty dollars on a card game if the winning hand offered fifty dollars back? No one. Sixty dollars back? Still likely no one. Two hundred dollars? Now there might be some takers. When the likelihood of future wins is uncertain, the payoff has to be higher to entice bettors to take a chance. And the more uncertainty involved, the bigger the pot needed to warrant taking a gamble.

It's the same with discounting. The more uncertain a person is that her efforts to study or to save will pay off, the more she'll discount the value of the future rewards that require perseverance. Recent findings attest to just this fact. When a team of researchers led by psychologist Vladas Griskevicius compared discounting levels among people who were raised in environments that differed with respect to whether inhabitants believed the future offered good things, they found an interesting pattern. After having people from different socioeconomic backgrounds complete an economic decision task similar to ours, they found that those who reported coming from a background of scarcity — one where they reported never being sure that their family would have enough money to meet its needs or desires — showed a marked increase in discounting future rewards when faced with the possibility of financial hard times compared with those who were raised in more financially secure environs. What's more, these results held even when the researchers took the subjects' present financial status into account, meaning that someone raised in a resource-scarce environment who was currently financially stable still discounted future gains more than did an equally financially stable person raised in an economically secure home.

A similar logic likely applies to the link between perseverance and growth mindsets — a term Stanford psychologist Carol Dweck uses for a belief that effort can increase intelligence or related abilities versus a belief that such traits are fixed. Simply put, if a person believes that intelligence is fixed, why would she ever try to improve it? It's only if people believe that they'll reap rewards from efforts — that, for example, studying will make them smarter — that taking the risk of forgoing immediate satisfaction in order to hit the books makes sense.

This type of discounting — one sensitive to probability — was the type I meant when I said it could be a feature of our mental software. Sacrifice and hard work can and do make sense to the extent that they lead to something, irrespective of whether that something is getting into medical school, finding a good job, landing a spot in the Boston Symphony Orchestra, or achieving a better karmic rebirth. And since none of these future goals is guaranteed no matter how much sweat you put in, the reward has to be a big one to override impulses to relax in the moment or take an easy way out. As we'll see throughout this book, evolution didn't shape our minds to be virtuous; it shaped them to be adaptive. And being adaptive often means knowing when to save energy rather than pursue goals that aren't worth the effort.

There's still a problem, though. If discounting were perfectly adaptive, we wouldn't need self-control and grit to combat it. Our minds would accurately estimate when it's worthwhile to persevere in the face of difficulty or temptation instead of cutting our losses. We'd all be expert gamblers, knowing when to hold on to our hand and when to fold. We'd never procrastinate if it was going to cost us down the road. But life doesn't work that way, which brings us to the *bug* part I mentioned earlier. While some degree of discounting is perfectly reasonable, our minds tend to overdo it. We overly discount the value of future gains, often resulting in self-defeating decisions that limit our potential for success.

It might seem strange that a psychological mechanism can be both feature and bug. In truth, it's not that discounting is a poorly designed psychological mechanism; it's just slightly outdated. We now live in a world that presents options with greater levels of certainty than ever before. We know with greater confidence than our forebears that smoking, drinking, and eating high-fat and high-sugar foods will harm our future health. We can count on the fact that investing in a bond or insurance policy will prove profitable down the road. And we have data confirming that, on average, getting a college degree leads to better long-term financial outcomes. True, none of these is guaranteed. You might get hit by a car after swapping that doughnut on your plate for a spear of broccoli, or graduate in the midst of a recession and never reach your full earning potential. But for us, compared with our predecessors who didn't have access to binding financial contracts or antibiotics, the links between patience, perseverance, upward mobility, and future outcomes are clearer than ever.

Unfortunately, our mental calculators haven't received the appropriate software update because evolution adjusts such things much more slowly than society has adjusted risk. As a result, we don't always get the math right, giving too much weight to immediate rewards. Thus, our calculations of long-term value are usually inaccurate, leaving us to irrationally overvalue pleasure and rewards in the present, with turning down opportunities for a 400 percent annual return being a case in point. The same logic, of course, applies beyond the financial realm. We're just as likely to overvalue anything that, though fun in the moment, can come with a future cost.

THE EASY WAY OUT

When I talk about the related challenges of discounting and self-control, people often believe that these challenges apply to others more than to themselves. That is, they tend to think that while others may give in to temptation easily, they themselves aren't so corruptible. In truth, though, the possibility that any of us will take the easy way out is fairly high. All it takes to see how and why is the right situation.

For people in an experiment run in my lab in collaboration with psychologist Piercarlo Valdesolo, that situation took the following form. On a warm and sunny late-spring morning — the kind where the sun beckons us to picnic or play — people were on their way to the lab to take part in a study which they'd signed up for the week before, when the weather wasn't quite as enticing.

When they arrived, they were escorted one at a time through the lobby and into a small room containing a chair, a desk, and a computer. As each took a seat, a researcher told her that he was conducting two different experiments today. One — the photo hunt — simply required people to scan through pictures on a computer screen to find certain objects. It was short — only about ten minutes — and most people found it to be quite fun. The other experiment wasn't quite so fun. It required people to complete forty-five minutes of difficult logic problems.

As the researcher explained, he must ensure that an equal number of people complete each task. So in an effort to be fair and not unduly influence who completes which, he's developed a new way to assign people. Every other participant will get to be a "decider," who, as the name implies, has the responsibility of determining which of the two tasks — the short and fun or the long and onerous — she will complete. And because the numbers doing each have to be matched, deciders' decisions will, by extension, also determine which tasks the other half of the participants — the nondeciders — have to work on. In short, this means that each decider will be determining not only her own fate but also that of the next person to be called from the waiting room, who will get stuck (or blessed) with whichever task the decider didn't complete.

Each participant then finds out that she will be a decider. The fairest way to determine which task she was to complete is to flip a coin, so the researcher hands her a device that works like a virtual coin flip to help in her decision making. When she presses the button on it, either a green or red circle will appear on its screen. If the circle is green, it means she's assigned to complete the short photo hunt. If it's red, the long set of logic problems awaits her. Once the researcher is sure she understands how everything will work, he leaves her with the randomizing device to begin.

As she sits there alone in the room, she ponders what to do. As far as she can tell, there's no way anyone will know whether or not she actually used the randomizer — the researcher made this clear when he was demonstrating it. In fact, she won't even see him again, as from here on out, everything she needs to do will involve using the computer in front of her. If she just presses the key to start the short photo hunt, no one will be the wiser.

We expected that most people would predict that they'd do the right thing — that they'd have the self-control to use the randomizer and accept its decision. In fact, when Valdesolo and I asked more than one hundred people what they believed the correct course of action to be, we found something quite rare in psychological research: unanimity. Everyone, and I mean everyone, said that not using the randomizer to determine who got stuck with the onerous job would be dishonest and immoral. It would show a lack of virtue and a weakness of willpower. Yet when confronted with the actual, as opposed to hypothetical, choice — when sitting in that room with the opportunity to cheat and get away with it — fully 92 percent of our participants succumbed to the temptation. How they succumbed varied; we could tell, because unbeknownst to participants, we watched them through a hidden camera. Some people completely ignored the randomizing device, choosing simply to assign themselves the photo hunt. Others decided to use the randomizer, not once, but *multiple times.* If the red circle appeared, which we had secretly programmed it to do for the first few attempts, they'd hit the button again, and again, and again, until it finally came up green. Even though it was still cheating, eventually seeing that green circle somehow made them feel better — like their repeated "do-overs" were justified.

The high percentage of cheating surprised us when we first saw it, so much so that we wondered whether we had somehow run this experiment on a deviant bunch of people. To check, we repeated the experiment several times with different participants. But each time the findings were about the same. On average, 90 percent of our participants cheated. So while in theory it's possible that any one of us might be among the 10 percent who would have the self-control to follow protocol, it's much more likely that we're not.

Now, failing to flip the coin doesn't mean a person is inherently immoral. I'm sure that most of the people who acted selfishly in our experiments are generally solid, upstanding folks. Most of them are likely hardworking and fair-minded. But just because someone usually acts with honesty and self-restraint doesn't mean they *always* will. This experiment shows that under the surface, our minds are always calculating tradeoffs. Though everyone we asked said taking the good task for themselves would be an immoral act, almost everyone did it. The reason, as I noted before, is that the human mind works to optimize outcomes, and in cases like this one — cases where a person can get away with a short-term gain in time and enjoyment with little long-term cost to their reputation — the mind will push them to do just that.

Time after time, temptation after temptation, we all face this dynamic. And while under more familiar circumstances, the number of times self-control might fail, though substantial, wouldn't likely be 90 percent — that high number stemmed from our tweaking the situation to provide anonymity and thus lower perceived future costs to reputation — these findings clearly show that everyone's minds were calculating tradeoffs. What's more, most people were easily tempted into behaving in ways that, though pleasurable in the moment, went against their own moral codes. Put another way, these results show that almost all of us will fail to use self-control when the only ones to whom we're accountable are ourselves. In real life, the analogs are clear. It might be a child weighing the costs of cutting corners on homework so she can tell her parents she's done and get on her smartphone. It might be you yourself comparing the benefits of going to the gym versus relaxing on the couch watching TV after a hard day. Whatever the specifics, it all boils down to a momentary, frequently biased-toward-the-present calculation meant to compare pleasure now with pleasure later. It's a mental tug of war — that *should I or shouldn't I* hesitation — that's all too familiar and all too often ends in regret.

It's also a conflict that most of us assume can best be solved by using the cognitive mechanisms of executive function to overcome emotions that favor immediate gratification. That is, use force of will to beat immediate happy feelings of pleasure. In reality, though, that's not the way the battle was playing out in people's minds when offered the choice between a long, annoying task and a short, fun one. As we'll see in the next chapter, in this experiment, as elsewhere in life, emotional responses weren't working to hinder self-control; they were working to boost it.

2

The Problem with the Solution

Why Willpower, Executive Function, and Reason Set You Up for Failure

The problem with relying on executive function is that, much as with any executive, the system only works if he/she/it possesses certain qualities. To succeed, a CEO needs to be rational, reliable, and lead an indefatigable staff ready to surmount any challenges that pop up. And herein lies the problem. Not only do executive function and its cognitive underlings tire quickly, but they can't even be counted upon to always do the job we assign them. Sometimes the mental executive can rationalize problematic behaviors, leaving people defenseless just when they need self-control most. So why don't we fire this metaphoric executive? Simply put: history. He's got a long set of references recommending him.

CHASING SPINOZA

While much of the country was reveling in rediscovering its emotional side in the late 1960s and early 1970s, psychologists were embracing a different ethos in their research labs. In this era, hopes for the prospects of computer science, artificial intelligence, and computational modeling ran high. The old idea that the mind was best understood as a black box that simply responded to punishment and reward — a notion put forth by B. F. Skinner and his behaviorist ilk — had been replaced by a shiny new metaphor: the computer. The mind wasn't a blank slate, it was loaded with complex algorithms, with decisions and behaviors resulting from specific "programs." So while flower power unfolded on campus greens, behind the ivy-covered walls of psychology departments, the cognitive revolution — the brain as information processor — was all the rage.

Although the computer analogy was seductive, researchers of the era didn't delude themselves that the mind, like a computer, was a completely controllable, rational apparatus. To their consternation, they recognized that it could sometimes produce seemingly illogical results. Take discounting, for example. Such aberrations of logic were usually ascribed to errors caused by more "primitive" mental mechanisms such as emotions that, having once served a purpose in ensuring the survival of our ancestors, now often got in the way of the higher mental capacities that underlie reason and planning in the modern mind. For many scholars, emotion was almost vestigial — a bug in an otherwise optimized operating system whose influence needed to be corrected.

Work on the marshmallow test began in this intellectual milieu. So we shouldn't be surprised that early attempts to understand what made children successful at delaying gratification focused primarily on cognitive strategies — those related to overcoming, ignoring, or reframing emotional responses. The strategy kids used most often applied willpower to suppress their emotional responses. But as this technique often proved difficult and unreliable, Mischel's team investigated other methods, too. Distraction seemed to work at times. When the kids focused their attention on something other than the treats — by singing a song, playing with their fingers and toes, or even picking their noses — they were better at waiting. So, too, did a strategy known as reappraisal, in which the kids pretended the marshmallows were something less tasty, like fluffy clouds. In both cases, the children were diverting their attention away from the gooey, desirable features of the object by using executive function. The mental executive, like a boss ordering employees to stop checking Facebook, ordered the eyes, and thus attention, to ignore or alter the interpretation of what was desired most in the moment in recognition that doing so would bring double the satisfaction in the future.

These strategies, of course, aren't limited to children; they can work for adults too. When we feel willpower failing, we can distract ourselves from objects we want to buy, fatty foods we want to eat, or cigarettes we want to smoke. Likewise, we can use reappraisal to reimagine a scoop of ice cream as a ball of artery-clogging goop, thereby changing how we perceive its attractive features.

Such strategies appear quite logical. Striving to reach goals means first, to borrow Mischel's terms, using willpower to "cool" a "hot" desire for immediate gratification. If willpower is fading, have a plan B. Distract yourself from the object calling from the store window, and you'll pass by without being tempted to purchase it. Reappraise a glass of vodka as a glass of poison that will damage your liver, and you'll stick to your promise to drink less. This is a theory of self-control that feels right. At one time or another, we've all experienced an increase in excitement, a craving, a yearning to do something in the moment that might not ultimately be the best course of action. In response, we often try to reason ourselves down from it, to "cool our jets," in hopes of avoiding later regret. It's also a theory with a good deal of empirical support. Mischel's seminal work inspired numerous subsequent investigations that, as I noted earlier, have linked willpower and related cognitive strategies to patience, perseverance, and, as a result, success in many realms.

It's a view of self-control that's also backed by evidence from neuroscience. In one highly cited example, Harvard economist David Laibson and colleagues asked people to make intertemporal decisions — did they want $X soon or some value greater than $X further down the line? — while they were lying in an MRI tube. The goal of the study was to see how areas of the brain associated with emotional responses — areas referred to as the limbic system — and those associated with reasoning and executive control — parts of the lateral prefrontal cortex (LPC) — worked together to guide economic decisions. Laibson predicted that more impulsive financial choices, the seemingly irrational ones favoring rapid yet smaller payoffs, would be associated with greater activation in the limbic system, while those associated with greater patience would correlate with more activation in the LPC. As it turns out, this is exactly the pattern he found. Decisions reflecting a lack of self-control — the ones where people grabbed the smaller yet readily available amount of cash — seemed to occur most when the emotion system was more active in the brain. Likewise, decisions to wait for the better, long-term payoffs occurred when activation favored the cool, rational system.

Combine these findings with those on the role of executive function in grit, and it seems that a clear picture emerges. Suppressing or overriding emotional responses solves the problem of intertemporal choice — it leads to making better decisions, to perseverance, and ultimately to success. There's even fMRI imaging to prove it. And although it's a view now cloaked in the trappings of modern science, it's really nothing new. More than three hundred years ago the Dutch philosopher Baruch Spinoza captured what is now pretty much the conventional scientific wisdom: that "in their desires and judgments of what is beneficial, [people] are carried away by their passions, which take no account of the future or anything else."

To me, though, this view just couldn't be right. And I'm not alone. Through the centuries, some economists, ranging from Adam Smith to Robert Frank, have argued that certain moral emotions push us to value the future more than we normally would. And my thinking on this topic is indebted to their work. But it's quite true that this view has yet to be fully embraced. One reason is that the more commonly held view isn't entirely wrong. If the theory that reason can be used to overcome emotional desire had no basis in fact, it would have disappeared long ago. But I worry we're making a big mistake by continuing to accept this view without question. Here's why: just because a prediction turns out to be true sometimes doesn't mean it will be true every time. The question, then, centers on what to make of situations that appear to show the reverse. Ones, as we'll see, where emotions might lead to enhanced patience and superior outcomes. Would such findings constitute flukes, or would they necessitate a major rethinking of the original position? If they're systematic — if you can predict when and why they occur — then it's certainly the latter. So when it comes to self-control, I believe that the "emotions are bad; executive function is good" theory needs revision because if it were true, it would require that emotions almost always favor the desires of the moment, while reasoned analysis does the opposite. Put another way, it would mean embracing the belief that you can always trust the rational, conscious mind to use willpower and related tactics when you need to act virtuously. Unfortunately, this isn't the case.

TWO MINDS ARE BETTER THAN ONE

Ask any psychologist who studies emotions why we have feelings, and you'll get the same answer. Emotions exist for one purpose: to influence what happens next. They're akin to mental shortcuts. They help the brain predict and adjust to the challenges it's about to face. Emotions can change our physiology by modifying our heart rate or breathing to prepare us for aggression, escape, or competition. They can alter our attention to and perceptions of the objects around us so we can better focus on what matters. And, perhaps most relevant here, emotions can shape our decisions by tweaking our mental computations — they can change the value or probabilities we attach to things. In all cases, the goal is simple: to increase the likelihood that we'll be able to meet whatever challenges the world throws at us.

From my previous perch as editor in chief of the American Psychological Association's journal *Emotion,* I can testify to the vast amount of research demonstrating the usefulness of emotions. For example, disgust protects our health by compelling us to avoid eating spoiled food or coming into contact with disease and contamination. Anger and fear increase our vigilance for possible threats in our environs. As a given emotion comes online, it alters the brain's expectations, which, as a result, alters its subsequent calculations. If I'm feeling disgusted, it suddenly seems more likely that I should quickly avoid whatever substance is in front of me. If I'm feeling afraid or angry, my sense that the person approaching me is a threat goes up.

It's important to note that a perception or decision doesn't have to be objectively accurate in order to be useful. So while anger will make you more likely to expect aggression from the next stranger you meet, it can be helpful at times even if the perception is unwarranted. Think of it this way: if that person is indeed a threat, this expectation will serve you well, but even if he isn't, your readiness to lash out at him might still serve an end. In the world of evolutionary theory, it's better to be wrong than to be dead; some mistakes are more costly than others. Admittedly, it's also true that on average emotions will increase adaptive decision making if these states are experienced in the appropriate intensities and situations. If emotions are too intense (or too lackluster) and/or regularly experienced when they shouldn't be, it's a problem. And if that happens too often, it's a disorder. But in most instances, emotions do work to help us meet challenges successfully.

When it comes to self-control, the situation is more complex, as time becomes a factor. The decision that seems best in the moment isn't always, or even usually, the same as the one that will bring the most satisfaction in the future. Breaking a promise to save yourself from an onerous obligation might make your life easier now, but in the long run it will likely erode a relationship and deprive you of all the benefits that relationship brought you. In the moment of temptation, you're often going to experience a sense of desire — an emotional response centered on the joys of short-term gain. But this doesn't mean that you can't experience, or strategically call upon, other emotional responses that might counteract the initial one. Humans are emotionally complex creatures; we can, and often do, experience dueling feelings.

Having simultaneous or rapidly cycling emotional experiences working in opposition to each other makes sense for the same reasons we use conscious deliberation to analyze and choose between competing options. We need to determine which option — immediate pleasure or long-term reward — is better in any given situation. If you accept that emotions serve adaptive purposes, and that there is a necessity at times to favor long-term rewards over short-term ones, then it seems quite possible that certain types of emotions might exist that nudge the mind to favor future gains over immediate ones. Persistence, cooperation, and generally unselfish behavior have been necessary to our survival for millennia; they didn't begin when we developed the mental acumen to logically lay out our future plans. This means it's exceedingly likely that emotions have been guiding our decisions since long before we had the cognitive skills to imagine and reason about the future. There should, then, be emotions that combat discounting — that work to tip the balance of the mental scale back toward the ant.

When we make decisions of an intertemporal type, we use not one mind but two. Where one mind is driven by the intuitive and emotional mechanisms that carry out their work often outside awareness, the other — the mind with which we're subjectively more familiar — is driven by conscious deliberation. As a consequence, whenever you confront a choice that holds different consequences as time unfolds, both minds swing into action.

Take the notion of saving for retirement or confronting the boss. On the conscious level — that part over which people have insight and believe they possess some control — an obvious weighing is going on. *Yes, it would be fun to spend this month's retirement contribution on a vacation instead* or *it would be satisfying to tell the boss to go jump in the lake,* but we know that the pleasures brought by both decisions, though satisfying in the moment, could be fleeting. So in the moments available before deciding to act (or not), people try to objectively weigh whether either action is worth the consequences.

Although you likely don't realize it, the emotional mind is weighing the same options under the surface. Yet the ways it determines which options are better will be influenced by different factors: what you're feeling. If it's primarily emotions such as desire, sadness, or anger — feelings known to push people toward short-term concerns — impulsive behavior won't be constrained. Wants will be emphasized; you'll be nudged to buy your plane tickets or to let your boss know what you truly think of him. However, if your mind is experiencing emotions such as gratitude, compassion, or pride when temptations arise, you will be pushed in the opposite direction. These emotions, as we'll see in the next three chapters, encourage a long-term view, meaning that they'll change the mind's computations of what it values to favor future gains over present ones.

Although having two metaphorical minds might seem redundant if not paralyzing (recall that being "of two minds" about something means you're undecided), it's actually the kind of redundancy that makes the entire decision-making system more robust. Of course, there's only one brain, but that brain can process along several paths at once, meaning our decisions can — and very often are — influenced simultaneously by emotional and non-emotional factors. The interplay between these mechanisms — the "two minds" — ultimately determines what we perceive and how we act on those perceptions. For that reason, the two-is-better-than-one analogy makes good sense.

As I'll discuss in chapter 6, issues of self-control are relevant to all social species, and as a result, our primate forebears had to possess mechanisms that balance short-term gains for oneself, which often require selfish behavior, with sacrifices to help the group, which also pay off bigger dividends down the line to the group's individual members. And so our ancestors' minds came equipped with emotion-based mechanisms that encouraged sharing, cooperation, diligence, and the like. As the complexity of the human brain expanded through evolution, so too did its relevant non-emotional tools: the ability to become self-aware, to plan ahead by engaging in mental "time travel" through simulation, and to adjust the more automatic, intuitive responses of the older, emotion-based system. So we modern humans retain two systems that weigh our choices and inform each other about their preferences. Each system serves as a check on the other in an attempt to ensure superior outcomes. When they agree, the choice of action is clear and thus reinforced. When they disagree, conflict emerges. Success then relies on knowing which system to trust. And as we'll see, placing trust habitually in the mind's cognitive faculties isn't always a good bet.

BEGUILED BY REASON

In my experiment on cheating from the previous chapter—the one where most people unfairly chose to take an easier way out for themselves at a cost to another person—we can see just how readily self-control fails. The vast majority of people, if they believe they can get away with it, will choose to benefit themselves in the short term even if it goes against their moral code. When I described the experiment, I said that contrary to what many people might suspect, Valdesolo's and my hunch was that people were relying on reason and related processes of their mental executive to help them justify their choice. The first step in determining if we were right was to see how they might view the same selfish choice when made by someone else.

Toward that end, we repeated the experiment, but this time we had participants watch someone else cheat (here an actor playing the role of another participant). So while the real participants sat in a cubicle watching via hidden video as the actor decided whether to use the virtual coin-flipping device, all the while believing they were "in" on the experiment, the true experiment was unfolding with them as the subject. After they watched the actor decide to ignore the randomizing device and simply assign himself the more pleasant task, they recorded their evaluations of his behavior. At the end of the first experiment—the one where people assigned *themselves* to a task—the computer had asked a simple question: How fairly did you act? Now, in this second experiment, it asked them a slightly different one: How fairly did that person (that is, the actor) act? What we found was nothing short of hypocrisy. When people rated their own objectively selfish actions, they judged them to be moderately fair. They didn't give themselves gold stars, but they certainly rated their behavior as acceptable. However, when people rated the very same failure of self-control in someone else, they condemned it as decidedly unethical. In both cases, the acts of giving in to temptation to take the easy way out were identical; the only thing that differed was who was doing the cheating.

Not only will most people succumb to selfish behavior if they don't perceive a big cost to it, but they'll readily condemn someone else for behaving in the same way. Put slightly differently, most people will fail to use self-control to adhere to a moral standard, and then, perhaps most surprising, excuse their own actions. They'll not only give in to temptation, but afterward they will believe they had a good reason for so doing. As you can imagine, that can be a recipe for disaster when it comes to learning from one's mistakes.

As unequivocal as these findings were, we still couldn't determine the exact roles that reason and emotion played in the decision. Although most people would tend to assume that emotions drove this questionable behavior — that feelings pushed people to maximize their own enjoyment in the moment, with reason and related cognitive functions attempting somewhat futilely to use willpower to restrain them — Valdesolo and I held a different suspicion. Luckily there was a way to find out which view was right.

We ran the experiment a third time, but now with another important twist. It turns out that there's a pretty easy way to determine whether emotions or conscious reason is influencing a decision: pile on a cognitive load. This means "loading up" working memory — that metaphorical space in the mind where we think and reason about things — with junk. The logic is simple. If your cognitive workspace is occupied, your ability to use executive function and reason is diminished; you won't have the wherewithal to think about, let alone control, your mind's more automatic responses. As a result, your decisions are ruled by intuition and emotion.

So this time we made sure to occupy people's minds when we asked them how fairly either they or the "cheating" participant behaved. First we subjected them to the considerable cognitive load of memorizing a series of random digits that had just disappeared from the computer screen in front of them; then we requested their opinion of their — or the actor's — actions. Since they had to hold the digits in memory, they couldn't really reason much about the cheating behaviors. As a result, they usually blurted immediate and unvarnished responses. Their answers made clear that emotions weren't pushing people to take the easy way out; to the contrary, they were urging self-restraint. When people under cognitive load had to judge whether they acted fairly or gave in to self-indulgence, they disparaged their own selfish behavior in the same way that they disparaged the behavior of others. They knew they had given in to temptation, and as they felt that pang of guilt, they admitted to it.

Left to its own devices, however, the reasoned, conscious mind was covering its tracks. The mental executive, like many CEOs, had analyzed the situation at hand and ordered the most adaptive behavior: cheat. Remember, people in our experiment believed that no one would learn of their deceit, meaning that they also believed they would suffer no long-term cost to their reputations by choosing immediate gratification. Actually deciding to cheat, however, required them to tamp down their emotional responses. They had to override a sense of guilt that was advocating a nobler course of action — one that, under most circumstances, would lead to long-term gains in admiration and reputation even at the cost of short-term losses in pleasure. After all, in most people's eyes, seeing someone exert self-control and believing they're trustworthy are tightly linked.

Proving the point, work by Harvard psychologist Joshua Greene has shown that the very brain centers associated with cognitive control often underlie dishonest behavior. Using an experimental design similar to the one Valdesolo and I used, Greene had people report the accuracy of their predictions for coin flips while having their brains imaged in an MRI scanner. Greene's participants believed they were in an experiment meant to investigate accuracy in predicting the future. They had been told that to incentivize them to work hard in making their predictions, they would receive more money for more accurate predictions. There was one wrinkle in the experiment's design, though. Sometimes people had to report their prediction (that is, heads or tails for a given flip) and then witness the actual flip. Other times they made their prediction but didn't have to report it until after the coin was flipped. As you might surmise, the second condition allowed for lying; people could change their internal prediction (if they made one at all) to appear more accurate and thus earn more money. As with our experiment, people thought there was little if any accountability for cheating. Greene found that the cheaters, who could be easily identified by their statistically impossible accuracy (many around 90 percent), showed greater activity in prefrontal brain areas, exactly those that underlie cognitive control and suppression of more automatic, emotional responses.

In these examples, you can easily see one of the inherent, but often unrecognized, downsides of relying on cognitive processes to maintain self-control. In fact, research has shown that early advances in cognitive skills among young children actually make them more prone to lie to get what they want. University of Toronto psychologist Xiao Pan Ding and colleagues taught three-year-olds who were never known to lie how to reason about the mental states of themselves and others. That is, they helped kids become better able to figure out what other people might know about the kids' own thoughts and behavior and what aspects would remain hidden in a given situation. The kids who were taught how to reason about these things ended up lying to the experimenters more often while playing a guessing game than did the three-year-olds who hadn't been taught. In short, stronger reasoning and related cognitive skills helped these kids to win by enabling them to break rules more effectively.

So yes, executive function can squelch emotional desires meant to favor immediate gratification, but so too can it generate its own reasons for why we should pursue immediate pleasure. As the saying goes, *rational* is only one letter away from *rationale,* and that's exactly what we're seeing here. In my studies, cognitive processes not only overruled an emotional impulse for self-restraint but subsequently removed any lingering concerns about questionable behaviors. Remember, participants viewed their own failure to follow protocol as fair when they weren't put under cognitive load; it was only when the influence of executive function was removed that they recognized and admitted their own transgressions.

In the experiments, the job of the mental executive was clear: it focused on spinning a story, a justification, to explain why not using the randomizing device was acceptable. When we asked people why they'd cheated in assigning tasks, we heard things like "Well, I normally wouldn't have, but I was just so tired today that I had to," or "I was worried I might be late for something, so it was necessary," or my personal favorite, "I think the guy who was coming in after me looked like an engineering type who would like difficult word problems." So while choosing not to use the randomizer might be adaptive in terms of resources, our earlier survey of people showed that, prior to taking part in the experiment, everyone believed that just assigning the easy job to themselves went against their moral codes. Nonetheless the vast majority of people gave in to temptation to take the easy way out even though they felt guilty for doing so.

Here's where the whitewash comes in. If we're to continue to believe that we are virtuous people, our minds need to obscure our past failures of self-control. Hence, the creation of a *rationale.* The only reason why consciousness creates a justification when we fail is to foster the illusion that we can trust ourselves to do what's right in the future. If we're going to believe we can save our money, control our eating, and work hard, we also have to believe that when we fail to do such things, there's a good reason — a reason that has nothing to do with indulging our own desires to gain immediate pleasure. If we don't believe this, we're in big trouble, as why would we sacrifice and persevere now if in the future we're likely to give in to temptation and act in a way that makes our current efforts worthless? In some ways, then, this whitewashing can serve a purpose. By deluding us into thinking that we usually act in accord with our moral code, it can, somewhat perversely, make it more likely that we'll continue to do so in the future despite letting us indulge in the sins of the present. But it's no sure bet. Often, it can do just the opposite.

Because reasoning isn't objective, the "mind as computer" analogy that was initially so popular with psychologists doesn't really fit. We frequently bend reason to suit our needs and to justify our actions in the moment. In fact, as work by psychologist Sonya Sachdeva has revealed, we're often willing to act most selfishly right at the time we're feeling most positively about our moral bona fides because we feel we deserve an indulgence. We'll let ourselves get away with behavior that's not quite admirable precisely because we think we're usually quite good; one small indulgence won't knock us down too much on the scale of virtue. Take that logic and apply it to studying, spending, eating, and the like, and you'll immediately see the threat it poses. Our minds are more than willing to believe that giving in to temptation is the right course of action, especially if we think we can get away with it, just like the participants in all these experiments. So while attempts to whitewash our failings can be useful when infrequent, if and when allowed to happen regularly, they can inhibit the pursuit of goals that require perseverance in the face of difficulty.

Once we recognize that reasoning can be biased, and that cognition is just as susceptible to short-term desires as is emotion, we can see the folly of assuming that executive function is always the best route to self-control and success. While cognitive mechanisms can certainly foster self-control, they only do so when *they* want to. More often than we'd like, these mechanisms convince us that not doing the right thing is actually the right thing to do.

DIMINISHING RETURNS

Even when willpower succeeds in fostering self-restraint, its effectiveness is limited by another factor: time. The notion that willpower can weaken with repeated use might seem counterintuitive at first. After all, many cognitive skills such as problem solving and memory can improve with practice. Willpower, though, is different. It takes great effort to use, meaning that it can result in a somewhat perverse effect: the more you use it without a rest in between, the more likely it is to fail. This isn't because willpower is a finite resource that can be depleted, as some have argued, but rather because directing executive function at specific tasks has inherent costs that can multiply over time.

When you're focusing your mental energies toward one demanding task, you're reducing the effort you can aim at others. As your mind continually updates the perceived tradeoffs of targets for its efforts, tasks whose rewards remain far in the future come to *feel* harder compared with others that offer more immediate benefits. The normal result is that unless future rewards have an extremely high value — a fact itself that is hampered by the discounting glitch — working toward them feels more onerous as time goes on, making failures of willpower more probable with each passing minute. Many experiments confirm this general pattern. To give you a sense of the general phenomenon, let's take a look at what is perhaps one of the most famous: the radish experiment.

Based on the name alone, you might assume this is some twisted take on the marshmallow test. And you wouldn't be far off. It was designed by University of Florida psychologist Roy Baumeister, who had a hunch that many failures of self-control stem not from an underuse of willpower but from an overuse. Maybe you're good at getting up early to go to the gym. At work you manage to control your temper when your boss angers you during a meeting. When you get home, you force yourself to study for an exam you plan to take. But then, as you pass the refrigerator, you hear a pint of ice cream calling out to you, and you suddenly realize, as you're on your third scoop, that you have nothing left with which to resist. It's kind of like that.

To examine his hunch, Baumeister's research team invited people to their lab to take part in what was billed as an experiment on intelligence. As the participants entered, they were seated near a table on which rested a plate of warm cookies, a few pieces of chocolate candy, and a bowl of radishes. The researcher told them it would be a few minutes before the materials for the session were ready, and invited some to eat the sweets and others to eat the radishes. Just to make sure that everyone was hungry and would be especially tempted by the sweets, people had been instructed to fast for several hours prior to their arrival. The experimenter then left the room and watched the unfolding events on hidden video to see what participants would do.

Those lucky enough to be in the "treats" group happily sampled the cookies or candy. Those in the radish group, like the successful children in Mischel's marshmallow test, looked hungrily at the treats but, as instructed, resisted the temptation to eat them. Some nibbled a radish after savoring the smell of the cookies, but none appeared happy about it. After a few more minutes, the researcher returned and escorted participants into another room, where they were set to work trying to solve what, unbeknownst to them, were unsolvable geometric puzzles. Baumeister wasn't actually interested in people's performance on the puzzles; he was interested in their perseverance.

Those who were invited to eat the cookies spent about twenty minutes on average working on the impossible puzzles. But those who had earlier relied on willpower to refrain from eating the treats gave up in less than half the time. The results weren't due to any burst in blood sugar, as the idea that caloric energy buffers self-control has been scientifically confirmed to be false. Nor did it appear to result from any change in people's moods after eating cookies. Rather, these findings stand as one of many that have shown the effectiveness of willpower to decrease when people face rapid-fire temptations. Similar work by behavioral economist Dan Ariely has shown that using willpower to keep yourself on task is associated with an increasing likelihood that you'll engage in unethical behavior to benefit yourself in the moment. As with most scientific claims, though, it's important to note that there is some debate about whether this diminishing effect of willpower applies equally to all types of challenging tasks (for example, ones that take physical effort). But we do know for sure that when it comes to tasks that require continued perseverance and performance over an extended period, the ability of willpower to keep people focused and working toward their goals certainly declines. Each success reduces the likelihood of continued mental effort aimed at self-control, making each subsequent use of executive function more difficult and less likely to succeed. So it would seem that the system many of us rely on to sustain our efforts under pressure is anything but resilient.

A Candle in the Wind

Kathleen Vohs, a professor of marketing at the University of Minnesota's Carlson School of Management and a leading expert on self-control, closely examined the habits of those who appear to be masters of self-control and grit. After she studied people's behavior in their natural environs over several weeks, what she found was startling. Those who regularly seemed to have the most success in resisting temptation succeeded not because their willpower or executive function was superior to yours or mine but because they were better at avoiding temptations in the first place. You can't spend too much gambling at a casino if you leave your credit cards at home!

It is precisely because of willpower's inherent limitations that the other strategies I've mentioned were developed. Willpower failing? Distract yourself from what you want. Think about that doughnut not as a treat but as a greasy ring squeezing shut an artery. Know you're going to spend some extra money meant for retirement? Lock it up in an account that charges high penalties for withdrawals.

All of these techniques are based on the premise that self-control is fragile, like a candle in the wind. Willpower alone can't ensure that you'll delay gratification to the degree necessary to achieve your long-term goals. It will fail, and probably just when you need it most. Repeated temptations will weaken it, but so too will a host of other aspects of daily life. Stress, for one, hampers force of will, but even behaviors as common as making many innocuous decisions quickly (for example, should I wear a white shirt or a blue one?) can do the same. So people grasp for other cognitive strategies to shield the flame of self-control from the winds of temptation. The only problem is, even if you can protect the candle from those winds, it will burn out with repeated use anyway.

What's not well recognized, however, is that attempts to keep the flame of self-control burning, even when successful, hold unintended and often adverse consequences. Work by Stanford psychologist James Gross has shown that using executive control to suppress feelings and desires harms memory. When you are striving to work or practice hard by burying either your desires for pleasure or your frustration at having to do something difficult, you're not only reducing the willpower you'll have to face the next temptation, you're actually making it harder to learn whatever you're focused on in the moment! Your ability to encode new facts or remember old ones becomes compromised. When your brain suppresses your emotions, it can't do much else well. So while using willpower might keep you sitting still and focused, it doesn't help you achieve as much as you might otherwise.

Cognitive strategies such as willpower, reappraisal, distraction, and the like do work at times, but they're not optimal. In its current conception, self-control is built primarily on inhibition; it rests on mechanisms meant to override a problematic desire for immediate pleasure. Yet as we've seen, these inhibitory mechanisms are fairly weak. When taxed too much, willpower fails, sending us into a downward spiral, where each attempt at success increases the likelihood of subsequent failure. Tired? Stressed? Making too many decisions? You'll suddenly find it's all going south.

While using cognitive mechanisms to inhibit desires for immediate satisfaction can work, it's stressful and requires much effort — effort that can take a toll not only on the mind but also on the body.

In fact, new research reveals how potentially destructive this method of self-control can be. A team led by Northwestern University psychologist Gregory Miller found that although higher levels of executive-function-based self-control among young people from economically disadvantaged backgrounds were associated with greater upward mobility and superior social outcomes, they were also associated with premature aging and its associated maladies. Now, it's important to note that this effect didn't hold for young adults raised in better circumstances. It only occurred among kids from families often characterized by reliance on government support and lacking college educations. But these are exactly the kids for whom self-control is supposed to matter most — the kids who can use grit to achieve a level of success greater than that of their families. And this route to grit did work for them, but at a steep price. The researchers showed that the stress involved in cognitively managing self-control — not the stress from living in difficult conditions — meant that these kids wouldn't likely be able to enjoy the fruits of their labor for as long or as well as they had planned. Proving the point, DNA analyses showed aging to a greater degree among those who used cognitive strategies to get gritty than among young people from similar adverse environs who hadn't relied so heavily on executive function to achieve success.

Fortunately, there is a way to solve this problem: don't use willpower and executive function to squash Aesop's proverbial grasshopper; change the initial evaluation of the options so that the ant (that is, the future) is favored from the outset. If you can accomplish this feat, it means you won't have to rely upon executive function to guide self-regulation in an arduous way. To the contrary, gritty behaviors will tend to flow effortlessly.

Logical as this view may seem, scientists have been stuck on how to bring it to fruition. One possible route involves habits. Psychologically speaking, a habit is an automatic behavior — a response that is triggered by one or more specific cues in the environment. It's something you don't have to think about or tell yourself to do; you just do it when and where you should. When I enter my house, I take my shoes off. When I get on the train, I pull out my monthly pass for the conductor to see well before he even walks down the aisle. It's mindless, and that's the point. It takes no effort.

Habits can be trained for anything, including self-control. In a wide-ranging examination of the links between habits and success, psychologists Angela Duckworth and Brian Galla found that stronger habits accounted for the links between self-control and valued outcomes in many domains. For example, they found that better study habits, defined here as attempts to study regularly at a specific time and in a specific place, explained the link between better self-control and superior academic performance in terms of homework completion and resistance to engaging in leisure activities at the cost of studying. Habits worked in the health arena, too. Duckworth and Galla found that regular eating and sleeping habits enhanced self-control when people faced temptations in those areas (say, staying up late or midnight snacking).

But while habits are effective to a degree, they can't offset all the limitations associated with cognitive strategies meant to enhance self-control. Although habits are automatic in a sense, and thus are easier to enact, they are highly specific. Developing a good study habit doesn't help your ability to diet, exercise, or invest. We must learn specific habits to address each new challenge, or even relearn old habits when aspects of a normal challenge change (like learning how to study in a college dorm versus in a bedroom at home). The upshot is that habits can help us delay gratification without stress but in quite limited ways. To grow perseverance more generally, what we really need is a more general and easily applied strategy that weakens the power temptations hold over us from the outset.

SUCCESS FROM THE BOTTOM UP

The sturdiest route to enhancing self-control wouldn't require effort to change what we value and desire, it would do so unnoticed and unbidden. Herein lies the power of using emotions as tools. As I noted earlier, emotions exist for one purpose: to guide our decisions and behaviors efficiently toward adaptive ends. Emotions don't require conscious guidance and effort to work; they change our views automatically. Yet, in freeing ourselves from the illusion that cognitive mechanisms offer the best route to self-control, we have to resist succumbing to an equally simplistic alternative: the belief that reveling in our emotions — any emotions — provides the answer. The mistake of earlier theories lay in mapping virtue and vice onto cognition and emotion in a one-to-one way. If we're going to improve on our strategies, we can't make that mistake again. We need to recognize that certain emotions will prove useful in delaying gratification whereas others will not. The trick, then, is to select the appropriate emotional tool for the task at hand.

To help us meet this challenge, the human mind comes equipped with an emotional toolbox of sorts. And in that box reside three specific emotions that will push the mind to value the future over the present. The strategies that use these three emotions have three advantages over those that use reason, habits, and willpower: (a) their strength doesn't wane after repeated use, (b) they can't be hijacked to favor immediate rewards, and (c) they improve our decisions in different areas of life at the same time. For example, when pride increases our willingness to persevere (as you'll soon see), it automatically makes us value future rewards more than fleeting ones, whether the long-term gains be musical skill, academic success, or promotion at work. What's more, this benefit is much broader in scope than learning a new habit. We don't have to develop one routine to succeed at studying and another to save money. Rather, evoking a specific type of emotion will create a general bias toward valuing long-term gains, which then bleeds over into many domains simultaneously. Likewise, feeling grateful or compassionate in one instance will affect decisions in several others.

Most important, these emotions will never steer you wrong. They exist for one purpose: to motivate positive social behavior. Because they're not based in executive function, they're immune to rationalization and bias. They can't be tweaked to fit the desires of the moment. Whenever we feel gratitude, compassion, or pride, it will only push our values one way: toward the future. As a result, they can be trusted. Unlike reasoning, these emotions won't work to subvert long-term goals by lulling us into a sense of complacency or expediency that we'll come to regret later.

Part 2

THE EMOTIONAL TOOLBOX

Gratitude Is About the Future, Not the Past

Gratitude might seem like the last emotion you'd select to help you plan for the future. With the possible exception of regret, no other emotion seems more focused on the past, or more passive in nature. In fact, if you ask most people why they feel grateful, they'll tell you it's because at some previous time, in whatever way, a person helped them obtain or achieve an object or a goal that they couldn't or wouldn't get on their own. While gratitude does involve showing appreciation for past actions and acknowledges that you can't always independently satisfy your desires, its true purpose is actually quite different. At a psychological level, gratitude isn't about the past; it's about the future. As we'll see, in preparing people to cooperate with others, gratitude changes what they value. It pushes people to work in the moment to benefit what is to come. In doing so, it's an extremely active state, not a passive one. Like all emotions, it influences decisions about what to do next.

Paying It Forward

Damn, now I have to get you something. Right there, that's the difference between feeling grateful and feeling indebted. Sometimes receiving a gift or a favor makes your heart swell with gratitude; other times it can lead to an annoying feeling of responsibility. How you value the gift or favor is the deciding factor. By value, I mean something based not on money or status but rather on a more flexible and intimate currency: care. I've experienced more gratitude for pictures and stuffed creations that my daughters spent hours hand sewing for me than I have for gifts worth hundreds of dollars. Likewise, I'm more grateful for specific moments when a mentor took time out of a busy schedule to give me advice than I am for receiving a recommendation letter that took a supervisor's assistant five minutes of cutting and pasting to produce. What unifies experiences of gratitude is the receipt of something one desires that comes at a cost to someone else. The art supplies my daughters used to make a gift for me cost pennies, but the time and effort they devoted were immense for eight-year-olds. A mentor putting his own needs on hold to talk with me about my concerns was more meaningful to me than a letter of recommendation with an impressive imprimatur.

We're grateful when we feel others have invested in us, which makes us willing to return the favor in the future. Sociologist Georg Simmel may have captured it best when he likened gratitude to the moral memory of humankind; it doesn't let you forget you owe someone something. Whether you're paying people back for their "investment" in you with money, time, or effort, gratitude nudges you to forestall or divert your own gains in the moment in the service of building or maintaining beneficial relationships for the long term. Think of it this way. A failure to show gratitude is often taken as an affront by someone who went out of their way to do something nice for you. And as affronts accrue, relationships die. That's why even if people don't truly feel grateful, there is a social norm to fake it: to say "thank you" and appear appreciative. But the real power of gratitude doesn't come only from its expression; it comes from its shaping of behavior.

This provides the perfect (and necessary) starting point to begin exploring gratitude's power to boost self-control. Just as gratitude helps us to overcome selfish temptations in dealing with other people, with a slight pivot it can also help us cooperate with a very specific person important to our long-term success: our future self. And at base, sacrificing immediate pleasure to help that person is what grit and related concepts are all about.

So if gratitude encourages cooperation through self-control, as I'm suggesting, we can make a straightforward prediction. When people feel grateful, they should devote more effort to help someone else, even if that help entails less than pleasant actions. That's the essence of cooperation; by definition, it has an intertemporal element. According to this view, you suck it up and help your friend move his furniture to a new apartment even though you'd rather spend the day at the beach because you're grateful for similar sacrifices he made to help you in the past. That gratitude you're feeling in remembering his help makes it easier for you to value his long-term friendship over the immediate pleasures offered by sun and surf. However, actually proving that this is the case — that feelings of gratitude encourage people to resist urges to loaf or to renege on commitments — requires running experiments with grateful people. And getting people to feel grateful when and where you need them to involves a bit of creativity.

If you want to know how gratitude truly affects people, you can't ask them. More than a decade of work by psychologists Daniel Gilbert and Timothy Wilson has shown that not only are people poor at accurately predicting what they'll feel in response to future, hypothetical situations, they're even worse at guessing how those feelings will affect their decisions. So asking someone what they'd do if they felt grateful is a scientific dead end. Examining how an emotion impacts decisions requires getting people to feel that emotion in real time and then seeing what they do when true costs and benefits — time, money, et cetera — are on the line. As I just noted, though, that often poses a problem: How do you make people feel grateful in the confines of a research lab?

This is the question with which we struggled. The first thing my collaborator, Monica Bartlett, and I considered was probably the most obvious: give people gifts. Unfortunately, that idea fizzled fast. It's almost impossible to think of a single gift that everyone would see as valuable both in terms of its desirability and our efforts to provide it. More people than you might guess don't really want a $15 Starbucks or iTunes gift card. So we had to retreat to a tactic we often use in the lab: the setup. Using a modified version of the method we used to study cheating — the one where people were told they had to complete either a short, fun task or a long, difficult one — we brought people into a room two at a time. One was a true participant, the other an actor who worked for us. After hearing about the two tasks, we had the actor volunteer to complete the onerous job. We thought the participants should feel grateful. Nope. They just felt lucky.

We ultimately realized that for people to feel grateful in this setup, they first had to get stuck with a problem; they had to own it. Only after that, when they were feeling the despair, could someone elicit gratitude by swooping in to help them out of their predicament. And so the third time was the charm. We devised a ploy where we placed our participants on the precipice of misery, only to be saved by the efforts of another. Well, maybe not exactly misery, but on the precipice of frustration to say the least.

Using a little creative computer programming and stagecraft, we brought people into our lab two at a time and sat them down in adjacent cubicles. One of the two was an actual participant, the other a confederate. We then set them to work completing a computerized task that we designed specifically to be long and boring. At the end of the task, we led people to believe that their score would appear on the computer monitor for the researcher to record. The only catch was that, unbeknownst to the participants, the computer they were working on was rigged to crash right as it was supposed to be calculating the final score. When it did so, there was always an audible groan or expletive that brought the participant's plight to the researcher's attention. At this point she'd inform the participant that unfortunately he'd have to redo the onerous task in its entirety — a pronouncement that usually brought on more groans or expletives.

The participants believed themselves to be stuck; they were in for another twenty minutes of effortful tedium. Now we had to make them grateful, and that required someone helping them avoid the drudgery they believed lay ahead. Luckily, there was just such a someone sitting in the next cubicle (the confederate). Upon getting up to leave, as her computer didn't have technical issues, she stopped, looked at the true participant, and said something like "Yikes. That's terrible. My computer didn't crash. I wonder why yours did? Hmm." She'd look at her watch. "I do have to run to my campus job, but let's see if I can help figure this out. I'm pretty good with computers." She'd then start playing with the cords and keyboard, during which time she would surreptitiously hit a key to start a countdown for the computer to come back to life. When it did, you could usually see the gratitude on people's faces. And to back it up, the relieved souls almost always reported feeling a good deal of gratitude when we subsequently measured their emotions.

Believing the experiment was now over, grateful participants left the lab and headed to the building's exit. But before they got there, we made sure that they'd come upon the person who had helped them fix their computer a few minutes before. This confederate, who now appeared to be collecting data for a class project of her own, would ask approaching participants if they could help her out. She needed people to complete a bunch of psychological tests. If they agreed, she'd sit them down to work in a room, saying the more time they were willing to devote to completing the tedious tests, the more help it would be. When they were done, all they had to do was leave their work in a folder.

Putting the logistical intricacies of the experiment aside, what we have is a very straightforward and commonplace dynamic. A person had helped our participants get out of a jam — a favor for which they felt grateful — and now was requesting their help, which would require perseverance to complete a difficult task. What's also important here is that participants' efforts to help weren't being monitored in real time. Although afterward it would be obvious how much work they had done, no one was sitting over them with a critical or encouraging eye. How much they worked was completely up to them.

When we compared the amount of time grateful people spent working to help the confederate with that spent by people in a neutral emotional state (that is, people who did the same experiment but didn't have their computer crash), we found a dramatic difference. Those who felt gratitude made more effort to help their benefactor; they spent 30 percent more time working on the tests. In fact, gratitude was directly linked to perseverance in a dose-dependent way. It wasn't simply knowing that someone had previously helped them that led people to work harder. Rather, it was the level of gratitude they felt in response to that help; as their level of gratitude increased, so did their efforts and time on the task.

Although this finding was encouraging, we had a nagging worry: it was possible that people helped the confederate not because they were grateful but simply because they felt they owed her a debt. To check whether it was truly gratitude rather than a basic sense of indebtedness that mattered, we ran the experiment again but with one simple change. Now the person who asked participants for help as they were leaving the building wasn't the person who had previously offered help in the lab but a complete stranger (that is, an actor working for us). As we expected, the same pattern emerged. People who were feeling grateful as they left the building were not only more likely to agree to help the stranger but spent significantly more time doing so than did people who weren't feeling any emotion in particular. So it surely wasn't the case that people were devoting more effort to help in order to pay back a debt to someone. They didn't owe this stranger anything; they had never seen her before.

As in the first experiment, the self-control that underlay effort was also dose-dependent. How long people persevered on the tasks meant to help the stranger was directly tied to how much gratitude they reported feeling at the moment she asked for their assistance. Those who had benefited from the confederate's actions in the lab but who weren't now feeling as grateful for some reason didn't work as long to help. Less gratitude meant less motivation to sacrifice time and effort.

Taken together, the findings of these experiments are somewhat remarkable, at least in respect to the current view of self-control. They show that experiencing an emotion — not ignoring or suppressing it — can lead people to work harder to benefit another. The more grateful people were, the more they helped — the more willing they were to accept short-lived costs in terms of their time and effort in order to help another. In the usual situation — one where gratitude and subsequent help are aimed at a previous benefactor — this dynamic makes great sense. Yet gratitude, whenever we feel it, ramps up our willingness to be future-oriented — to work to help anyone. Here it becomes easy to see that gratitude really isn't so much about paying back as it is about paying forward. From a biological standpoint, the reason we pay back isn't really because we're indebted. If you're not going to see a person again, the most adaptive decision is to cheat him. You'd be ahead. But if you are going to cross paths with him again — something that usually occurred in our ancestral environs — you'd have to deal with the shadow of the future, and that means behaving fairly so that you can continue to accrue the benefits that come from relationships with others.

Few have highlighted the important role giving plays in success as well as Adam Grant of the Wharton business school. In his well-known analysis of givers versus takers — people who are willing to devote time and effort to help others versus those who benefit from help but refuse to return the favor — Grant shows that on most every metric of success imaginable, givers, over the long haul, come out on top. Yes, as in most cases, there can be too much of a good thing; giving repeatedly and unconditionally can make you a doormat. But outside of such an aberrant case, generosity ensures that you'll be valued and paid back in spades. One major benefit of gratitude, then, is that it offers perhaps the fastest and easiest route to instill a readiness to give — one that does not rely on force of will and resists being subverted by motivated, selfish reasoning. And in so doing, it focuses our minds and actions on what lies ahead.

MAR$HMALLOW REDUX

Up to now, I've been showing how gratitude can build self-control when giving to others. And while these behaviors surely sound as if they'd require some degree of self-control, there's a slight difference in focus. In the previous examples, people were using self-control to help another — not themselves — succeed. I've pointed out that in helping others we also help ourselves down the line, and that's certainly true. Less obvious but equally true is that gratitude can help us help ourselves via a different route: by directly helping our own future selves.

In all cases, successful cooperation with a partner requires an ability to resist an immediate temptation to cheat or loaf. When you study for a test rather than play, save money rather than spend it, or eat broccoli rather than candy, what you're really doing is ensuring that future you will be better off. She'll be more likely to get into college and less likely to run out of money or get cancer. But making this happen costs. It means present you has to forgo some immediate satisfaction. As in any delayed exchange, one person has to give something up front in order to reap later benefits.

The most common way people try to solve the cooperation problem between their present and future selves is to rely on reason and willpower. But this technique doesn't always work so well. Just as most people are willing to cheat others if they believe they won't get caught — remember the 90 percent who regularly did so in my experiments — the same is true when it comes to cheating one's future self. In fact, it's probably easier to act in a selfish manner toward someone you know you'll never face — future you — than it is toward someone who you might possibly encounter again next week. Future you will forgive you for spending, partying, or indulging anyway, right? The answer, unfortunately, is probably *yes,* as we've seen evidence that most people tend to rationalize their sins away.

What's really needed to solve the problem is a more reliable instrument than executive control. As we've just seen, gratitude made people willing to sacrifice to help *anyone;* it functions like a constant nudge to value the possibilities the future holds. And as a result, my team thought it might easily and reliably foster cooperation with one's future self, too. If we were correct, gratitude should facilitate self-control in waiting for the proverbial second marshmallow.

To put this idea to the test, we set out to examine gratitude's effects on self-control in adults in the same way Mischel examined self-control in children. But there was one small problem: most adults don't covet marshmallows. Most do, however, like cash. So we employed a cash-based technique typically used by economists to measure self-control: decisions between receiving smaller amounts of money now and larger amounts later. If you remember, in chapter 1 I described how we used this strategy to demonstrate that most people overvalue the present; they were willing to accept $17 in the moment to forgo $100 in a year even though that stellar rate of return is unheard of in the financial industry.

To see if gratitude might increase patience, we repeated this experiment, but now with two different types of people: happy and grateful. The reason for including happiness was to be certain that any benefits we found with gratitude weren't simply due to people just feeling good. After all, happiness and gratitude are both positive states. If there were something special about gratitude, we needed to show that its ability to enhance self-control didn't mirror that of any pleasant emotion. And because we were also interested in finding ways to induce gratitude that, unlike our usual method involving actors, could work outside the lab, we relied on a simpler strategy this time: we had people reflect on events from their lives that made them feel grateful or laugh out loud (that is, happy) right before they indicated their financial preferences.

The results were impressive. Whereas people who were feeling rather neutral showed the usual impatience, those feeling grateful were significantly more future-oriented. It took $31 to tempt them to forgo the $100 future reward compared with the $17 neutral folks were willing to accept. What about those feeling happy? Their level of impatience was indistinguishable from that of the neutral people; they'd take the pleasure $18 could buy them now rather than wait a year for $100. This finding, perhaps more than any other, reveals the importance of distinguishing between the effects of specific emotions when it comes to self-control. Merely feeling good didn't make people more patient. Neither did inducing any old emotion distract them from their desires. No, it was something specific to the class of emotions to which gratitude belongs — the one focused on building and maintaining interpersonal bonds.

As important as this finding is, it offers a single snapshot into people's decisions. If I'm going to argue that cultivating gratitude will enhance self-control in our lives, it's also important to see whether it provides a constant buffer against the temptation for immediate gratification in day-to-day experiences.

Examining this question required conducting a yearlong study during which we followed waves of participants for three weeks at a time using mobile technology. For our participants, unlike for us, it was a pretty easy gig. All the study required people to do was, at the end of each day, report how often and to what degree they'd experienced several different emotions. After three weeks of reporting, we asked people to complete the monetary preference questions we always use to assess impatience. The data revealed exactly what we had hoped. Differences in daily levels of gratitude were strongly associated with self-control. To get a sense of how much gratitude mattered, people who experienced about 33 percent more gratitude than their average peer during the three weeks evidenced double the financial self-control compared with those who experienced about 33 percent less than the average peer (that is, annual discount factors of .33 versus .21).

Taken together, these findings offer clear proof that feeling grateful does nothing less than increase our willingness to wait for or persevere toward a greater, future reward. Of course, feeling grateful didn't perfectly solve the problem of self-control; it's not as if discounting completely disappeared, nor should it be expected to. But for simply inducing gratitude through reflecting on a past event to increase annual discount factors to this degree is a rather profound occurrence. Think of it this way. If you ask any financial planner how much of your annual salary should be put aside for a comfortable retirement, you'll likely hear an answer of about 15 percent. And in our experiment we saw that a simple evocation of gratitude was all it took for most people to raise their valuation of the delayed versus immediate rewards by 14 percent. Now, I'm not saying that how much money people save is solely a function of self-control. There are many other economic variables involved. But I am saying that for expendable income — whatever that might be for any given person — any factor that could encourage even modest increases in savings could make a huge difference in future well-being.

Equally important here is that unlike willpower or other cognitive techniques, gratitude didn't appear to require much effort. We didn't see our participants struggle with their decisions. This observation jibes nicely with recent findings by University of Toronto psychologist Michael Inzlicht, which showed that gratitude doesn't work by modifying executive function or conflict monitoring. That is, it doesn't work by strengthening willpower or related cognitive techniques meant to override or distract us from present temptations. Instead, it makes future goals more attractive, thereby easing the way to decisions favoring the future.

CONSUMPTION, COMMITMENT, AND COMPETENCE

If gratitude truly can help solve the problem of self-control, it has some pretty broad implications. If we're talking about high school students, for example, those who are regularly more grateful should have better social lives, better GPAs, and better spending habits, as saving money, getting good grades, and forging strong relationships all arise from patience and sacrifices that stand to benefit us in the years ahead.

So, for a moment, picture high school students from an affluent suburb of any major city. What words come to mind? I'd hazard a guess that among them are *driven, stressed, materialistic, status-aware,* and *grade-conscious.* It's not surprising that worries about getting into college and finding a career lead many teens to be anxious. Likewise, it's no surprise that one driver of this worry is a growing materialism among many adolescents that has continued unabated for decades. Of course, just as high school students vary in their grades, so too do they vary in their stress level, spending habits, and social support. They also vary in how much gratitude they typically feel.

In line with the view I've been advancing here, work by Jeffrey Froh, a psychologist at the University of California at Berkeley, attempted to tie these factors together to see why some students at a large high school on Long Island were doing better than others. He surveyed more than one thousand students, collecting data on their GPAs, levels of gratitude, depression, materialism, life satisfaction, focus, and social integration. He found exactly what you'd suspect if gratitude supported self-control. On the social side, gratitude was an exceedingly strong predictor of the teens' social bonds and their life satisfaction. Those who regularly experienced more gratitude had higher-quality relationships, greater joy in spending time with friends and family, and felt more supported by their communities. They also felt less depressed and envious of others.

Regarding academic success, the story was much the same. Being more grateful in daily life was associated with not only higher grades but also with more frequent experiences of enjoyment in the pursuit of academic goals. Although this sort of enjoyment may not sound exactly like self-control, the two are closely related. The more a future goal is valued relative to immediate pleasures, the more we typically enjoy working toward it. We don't feel the urge to pull away, as our mental calculations continue to suggest that the short-term sacrifices are worth it. As a result, we may not even feel that the effort needed to persevere toward a goal is a sacrifice at all. And although Froh's work is correlational in nature — it shows that increasing gratitude was associated with superior academic performance without being able to prove that one caused the other — I believe, based on the other evidence we've seen to this point, that gratitude likely was a cause. By focusing people on the future, whether or not they consciously realize what's going on, gratitude removes temptations to divert attention elsewhere and builds success by helping people remain committed to their long-term plans.

People in any profession that requires ongoing effort and engagement can benefit from gratitude. A wonderful example comes from the medical world. Physicians, especially younger ones, are routinely overworked, which poses a rather big problem given that their days are filled with complex diagnoses and decisions. Toward the end of long day or a bad week, it can be tempting to arrive at a quick decision rather than put in the time and mental effort needed to best diagnose a patient's problem. Doing so, though, holds long-term risks not only for the physician's reputation as a diagnostician but unfortunately also for the patient.

Cornell psychologist Alice Isen wondered whether good feelings from gratitude might remove the temptation of physicians who are feeling burned out to give decisions about their patients' problems short shrift. She designed a study in which she gave internists a folder containing information about a fictitious patient's medical history, physical exam, and lab results typical of those used to form an initial diagnosis. Next, she asked them to decide what might be ailing the patient. Just before reading the files, however, she gave some doctors a bag of candies as a gift (which they weren't allowed to sample until after the experiment) while asking others to read a set of humanistic statements about the practice of medicine. The first was meant to induce a mild dose of gratitude, the other to reinforce notions about treating patients well. What transpired next was exactly opposite what you'd expect if emotions always hindered self-control. Doctors who were feeling grateful for the kind gesture were not only more likely to arrive at a correct diagnosis, but they did so by spending more time gathering and accurately processing relevant information from medical records than did the ones who were reminded about the importance of treating patients with care. In short, the grateful doctors devoted more effort to doing their job, and doing it well, simply because of a small change in their emotional state.

Self-control, however, isn't always about working harder or smarter; it also plays a role in spending wisely. As my work showed, gratitude made people more financially patient. Supporting this view with choices outside a lab, Froh's research on teens confirmed that those who experienced gratitude more frequently also tended to be less materialistic in their purchases. They made fewer impulse buys. Interestingly, the benefits of gratitude didn't end there, however. Grateful teens' general happiness depended less on making expensive purchases than that of their less grateful peers. For the habitually grateful, happiness came from pursuing long-term goals as opposed to satisfying wants with markers of luxury. In fact, recent work by Cornell psychologist Thomas Gilovich highlights the link between gratitude and decreased materialism. In surveying more than twelve hundred randomly selected comments from consumer websites (for example, *TripAdvisor, Yelp, Amazon, CNET*), Gilovich's team found that feelings of gratitude were mentioned more frequently when the purchase was an experience shared with others as opposed to a material object.

GRATITUDE DOES A BODY GOOD

Given gratitude's ties to self-control, it should come as no surprise that it can benefit your health as well as your work and wallet. This is because many health-related decisions are intertemporal in nature.

Smoking may be very enjoyable in the here and now, but there's no doubt where it leads. The same with eating junk food or watching television instead of exercising. But there's emerging evidence that feeling grateful can give our mind the boost it needs to resist temptations that can harm our health. For example, increased gratitude is associated with less use of tobacco and alcohol. Likewise, it helps motivate people to eat well and exercise to improve their health.

Perhaps the biggest benefit of gratitude in the health domain is its effortlessness. As we've seen, traditional routes to self-control can be quite taxing on our body as well as our mind. Even when they work, they cause stress. Employing gratitude, though, heals and supports the body and mind while simultaneously helping us make healthier decisions.

A wonderful example of this shoring up of physical resilience can be seen in research by Wendy Mendes, a professor at the University of California at San Francisco Medical School. Mendes, who is known for her work examining physiological responses to stress, wanted to see if and how gratitude can buffer the negative effects of stress on the cardiovascular system. To find out, she adopted a commonly used scientific strategy to stress people: the Trier social stress test. At base, the Trier puts people into a potentially anxiety-provoking, and unfortunately familiar, situation: the oral presentation. One by one, participants appear in front of a panel of evaluators to deliver a speech that they've only had a few minutes to prepare. As they talk, members of the panel (who are actually actors) sit stonefaced while listening intently. For most people, not getting any feedback during a presentation, whether verbal or nonverbal, is interpreted as disapproval. Expressionless faces imply boredom, disagreement, or worse. And so for most people the Trier amps up stress a good deal. It has been shown to elevate levels of stress-related hormones in the blood (cortisol and ACTH) as well as cardiac activity and blood pressure, all in addition to increased self-reports of anxiety and related negative feelings by those involved.

In situations like the Trier, self-control can determine whether people melt down or persevere. Actively monitoring a presentation and feedback to it requires people to pay attention and correct for any errors, while trying to look smooth and engaged. The question for Mendes's team was: Do people who typically feel more gratitude show less physical wear and tear while enduring the Trier test? Mendes wired her participants up with mobile sensors to monitor their blood pressure while they faced the unfriendly panel. What emerged was a direct correlation between chronic levels of gratitude and people's stress responses. The blood pressure of those who experienced gratitude more often in their daily lives was less reactive to the stressful situation. Simply put, the extra effort they used to manage the situation didn't tax their cardiovascular system as much. Elevated gratitude also corresponded to lower blood pressure at rest (that is, before facing the panel). These findings suggest that throughout their daily lives, people who feel gratitude more regularly won't only have lower blood pressure levels in general but will also tend to show smaller spikes in blood pressure under stressful situations. The result is less wear and tear on the cardiovascular system.

Mendes's team has also found evidence linking elevated gratitude to higher levels of good (HDL) cholesterol and lower levels of bad (LDL) cholesterol, which likely result from a combination of lifestyle choices in exercise and diet. The more people are willing to hit the weights or skip the fries, the better their lipid profiles will be. Even inflammatory biomarkers, another important indicator of disease progression, are associated with gratitude. The more regularly people feel grateful, the less inflammation they show, again pointing to this emotion's buffering effect against stress.

The health benefits of gratitude also extend to the mind. People who feel grateful more frequently show decreased anxiety and depression as well as increased optimism. These benefits also likely explain gratitude's positive effect on sleep. Mendes's work along with that of others confirms that more feelings of gratitude during the day lead to a more calm and blissful sleep at night for the grateful person *and* for his partner; better sleep for one means less restlessness to disturb the other.

Suggestive and surprising as these findings are, they are correlational in nature. That is, they show that higher levels of gratitude are associated with decreased anxiety, better sleep, and the like; levels of one can be predicted using levels of the other. But unlike evidence from true experiments, they don't prove that gratitude *causes* increased well-being. It might be, for example, that people who have better social relationships tend to feel more grateful because of them, not the other way around. So while these findings are consistent with a causal view, it would be helpful to have evidence showing that changes in gratitude directly produce changes in measures of well-being. Or, put another way, to show that people who suddenly started cultivating gratitude showed positive changes in their lives down the line.

Fortunately, Robert Emmons, a psychologist at the University of California at Davis, took up this challenge. Emmons's team followed two hundred participants over nine weeks to see whether encouraging people to feel more grateful in their daily lives would benefit their health and outlook. Every few days he asked half the people in his experiment to write down and reflect upon a few recent incidents for which they were grateful. These didn't need to be major life events; they could be kindnesses as small as someone stopping to give you directions or a driver letting you get in front of her. He asked the other half to write down a few recent events in their lives of any type. The result was that he now had two groups of people who were reflecting on their lives but only one that was specifically counting their blessings.

After nine weeks it was clear that those who'd begun to cultivate more gratitude in their lives benefited from it. They not only exercised more — something that clearly requires self-control for most of us — but also reported better health, measured as fewer symptoms of illness (runny nose, upset stomach, sore throat), and general feelings of well-being. Here again gratitude's dual nature can be seen in its heightening of perseverance in health-related behaviors and its lowering of stress.

Spiraling Up

Resilient mechanisms are robust. By design, they're easy to use and they don't tax the larger systems in which they're embedded. Gratitude qualifies as such. Unlike willpower and related cognitive strategies, it's fairly easy to employ and doesn't come with physical costs. At a minimum, these facts imply that using gratitude won't increase the probability of entering a downward spiral as demands for self-control rise. However, emerging research suggests an intriguing and somewhat profound possibility: gratitude won't only avert a downward spiral, it might, unlike willpower, actually produce an upward one with repeated use; using gratitude to grow self-control actually becomes easier each time you do it.

The work in question comes from Indiana University neuroscientist Prathik Kini and colleagues, who imaged people's brains while having them play a pay-it-forward gratitude game. As the study participants lay in an MRI scanner, they saw images of other people who were giving them money as part of a game, which, of course, made them feel grateful. But the givers asked the participants to pay their gifts forward if and when an opportunity arose. And by design, the researchers frequently offered participants that very chance: to give some or all of their money to another person or to a favorite charity. One intriguing, but not altogether surprising, finding was that the more grateful people felt for a gift, the more active the reward centers in their brain became when they paid the gift forward. In many ways, this finding provides a neural basis for the effects of gratitude on behavior we've seen already. As in my studies on cooperation, feeling grateful increased people's readiness to accept a sacrifice and behave virtuously, even toward strangers. The neurological data suggest why: the grateful brain views giving as rewarding, which makes sense if gratitude increases the value we place on the future relative to the present, since biologically speaking, the act of giving usually results in greater benefits down the line.

The more interesting finding from Kini's experiment, though, is related to the feed-forward effects of gratitude. As it turns out, a few weeks before, half the participants in his study had engaged in an exercise meant to increase gratitude; they had spent time writing letters expressing their appreciation to previous benefactors. At the time Kini scanned their brains while they played the giving game, those who had done this previous task showed a different neurological pattern from those who had not. While everyone's reward centers became proportionally more active in response to how much gratitude they reported feeling, this effect was magnified among those who had previously completed the gratitude-inducing exercise. Not only did these people feel more grateful when playing the game, but their brains found it more rewarding. To put it bluntly, gratitude reinforces gratitude. The more often you experience it, the easier and more rewarding it becomes, and the more readily it enables self-control and its associated behaviors. It's the exact opposite of what happens with willpower; gratitude produces an upward spiral in efficacy, not a downward one.

Fortunately, we can grow gratitude in our daily lives pretty easily. Remember, emotions need not only *happen* to us. We have great power to determine what we feel. The brain isn't as much a response mechanism as it is a predictive mechanism. It's always guessing what's coming next based on what's come before. For example, whether or not the sound of breaking glass makes a person nervous depends on when and where she hears it. If she's eating lunch in a bustling bistro, the sound of glass breaking won't likely make her anxious, as it likely reflects a waiter's mishap. But hearing that same sound while lying alone in her bed at midnight might well produce a twinge of fear as her brain makes a different prediction for what's likely going on. The upshot here is that, in many ways, emotions constitute guesses about what's coming based on what has recently occurred. So all we need to do to change our emotions is to alter our mind's perceptions of what has recently happened. Put differently, we just need to tweak what we typically pay attention to.

The essence of any strategy to cultivate gratitude, then, is to focus on someone having helped us. The form that help takes (for example, financial, social, physical, informational) isn't important. What is central is that we appreciate their efforts, support, and kindness. While some people might worry that this strategy could limit achievement, as it emphasizes a weakness or inability on a person's part to achieve a goal on his own, we've just seen many examples that prove such a concern to be baseless. Humans are wired to repay others, and tapping into gratitude offers a way to channel that energy. The trick to fostering gratitude in daily life, then, is in how we appraise situations. In some of the experiments I've described, we nudged participants to appraise situations in ways that give them something to be thankful for. And in each case, greater self-control was the result.

As we've seen, one easy way to accomplish this is to count your blessings. It's a way to realize what others have done for you, and in so doing, to evoke gratitude. But in counting blessings, it's important to focus on the little things perhaps more than the big ones. Even a miraculous act of kindness can lose its emotional impact if we think about it every day. Reflecting on the smaller and more frequent ones — a modest bit of help from a friend or a coworker when needed — will work just as well. An easy way to make this strategy part of a routine is to keep a gratitude journal. Two or three times per week, don't only reflect on what you're grateful for, but write it down. The act of writing encourages a deeper, more vivid processing of memories, and can readily immerse us in the feelings brought forth.

Still, there are many people who report feeling that they don't have much to be grateful for. My friend Robert Frank, who is an economist at Cornell, notes that many people are uncomfortable with the possibility that their success wasn't entirely driven by them. That luck, or the actions of others, might have played a big role. And to drive the point home, he cites findings from the Pew Research Center and others that show a strong positive relation between income level and a tendency to believe that success comes from one's own hard work. Now, hard work certainly matters. If it didn't, I wouldn't be writing a book about how to increase perseverance. But it's equally true that success results from many causes, including the kindness and generosity of others and, often, even luck. As Frank points out, many people, and I happily include myself among them, can point to certain events that were integral to helping them reach their goals: getting excellent mentoring at a critical point in a career, having a parent or friend provide financial assistance to chase a dream, even simply being in the right place at the right time to land a job or internship that opened doors.

An important strategy for each of us, then, is to fight the common tendency to believe that our successes were completely self-determined. Unfortunately, this can become more difficult to do as our achievements grow, with the result being that the closer we get to our goals, the harder it can be to maintain gratitude. But by trying to remember objectively what happened — what factors besides our own efforts truly played a role — we can allow ourselves to feel grateful. Even luck can be reframed in this way. Yes, for some, being in the right place at the right time might simply reflect a statistical improbability rather than the hand of God interceding, but it's still a rare event and one that could have just as easily happened to someone else. Gratitude for good fortune is gratitude nonetheless. Reminding ourselves of this, and thereby allowing gratitude to rise even toward fate (as the human mind is ready to anthropomorphize any unknown force), can be a useful way of making this emotion part of daily life.

There's one more strategy I want to suggest before moving on. And unlike those I've described up to now, it's one that has the potential to involve many people at once: the reciprocity ring. Although there are many variants of it, the basic idea is straightforward. People, by writing on a board or putting up sticky notes on a wall in the shape of a circle, put forth requests for help with something, along with their names. Then people in the same group are encouraged to *find* a request that they believe they can assist with, and to write their name next to it. Finally, lines are drawn connecting people's names in the circle that indicate their two roles: requestors and assisters. What usually appears is a ring of sticky notes with many lines crossing through it — lines that visually represent a net of support — followed by behaviors to back it up. And the resulting support, of course, grows feelings of gratitude in the group.

For those who manage groups, whether in corporate settings or in classrooms, the usefulness of this technique is likely clear. In truth, though, it can work anywhere. A parent can post a reciprocity ring on the refrigerator for family members to fill out over several days. Any person living in an apartment building can post a ring on the building's community board. Offering assistance to someone else will undoubtedly result in others returning the favor, and thus future opportunities to feel grateful. It will also grow the gratitude of those in the immediate community, which, as we'll see later, can produce a resonance that reinforces everyone's success.

4

Compassion Builds Inner Strength and Inner Peace

Compassion, like gratitude, is intimately tied to social living. No man or woman is an island, meaning that in one way or another we all depend on our fellows. And whereas gratitude stems from recognizing that others have offered us something of value, compassion derives from the flip side. Simply put, it motivates us to care about others without having to have previously received help or benefits of any kind from them. As such, it starts virtuous cycles by encouraging people to take that first step to sacrifice time, money, or some other resource to benefit another, even if that other is their own future self.

To see an example of compassion's benefits in action, let's look at one of the biggest intertemporal dilemmas facing workers in major economies: retirement savings. It's a classic ant-versus-grasshopper problem. People can use cash in hand to satisfy an immediate yen, or they can put it in their slightly underfunded retirement account, which, if it remains underfunded, will result in a grim old age. Most people, as is evident from report after report on savings and expend-able income put out by the financial industry, will opt for the first choice: to forgo investing available income and, in so doing, disre-gard any suffering it might cause their future selves. People certainly realize the consequences of failing to save when they can; almost every employer and financial advisor makes the state of play abun-dantly clear. Nonetheless, and unsurprisingly, applying rational anal-ysis doesn't solve the problem, as it's not always strong enough to help most people avoid the temptation of pleasure in the moment.

Jeremy Bailenson, an expert in virtual reality, and psychologist Hal Hershfield thought that one way to help solve this dilemma might be to help people more easily empathize with their future selves. The underlying idea was quite straightforward: feeling more compassion for the future you should make it easier to resist eco-nomic choices that could leave that person in the lurch. The prob-lem, of course, is exactly how to increase such compassion. Future you is, after all, a stranger. You've never met this person face to face, and under normal conditions you never would. But the solution Bailenson and Hershfield concocted wasn't exactly normal.

Using face-modeling software, the team built three-dimen-sional models of what their participants, most of whom were about twenty years old, would look like at seventy. They then had their participants put on a virtual reality headset and enter a room for an interview with a virtual researcher. As people sat to be interviewed, they saw a mirror on the wall directly across from them, and in that mirror was a reflection of either their current face or the aged ver-sion. So as the interviewer asked them questions about their goals in life, they could see themselves answer as twenty-somethings or as senior citizens.

Following the virtual interview stage, the participants answered questions about what they would do if they were suddenly handed $1,000. Would they use it to buy something nice, put it into their checking account, plan a fun and extravagant occasion, or invest it in a retirement fund? Those who had just seen their future selves, and thus established a closer link with them, decided to allocate more than twice as much of the $1,000 to their retirement savings compared with those who hadn't ($172 versus $80). That's a huge effect! When the researchers ran the experiment a second time, using a temporal-discounting task similar to the one I've used, they again found that people who were helped via virtual reality to envision and empathize with their future selves showed greater self-control in the form of a lowered discounting rate: they valued future rewards more than did their peers.

To prove that it really was care and compassion for future selves that drove willingness to sacrifice in the moment, Bailenson and Hershfield made one additional tweak to their experiment. When they ran it for a third time, they allowed people to allocate more or less money to their retirement funds based on how happy or unhappy it made their present or future selves. To make those consequences clear, people could see the computerized images of either their present or future self's face — they only saw one or the other — change as they considered what to do with the cash they had in hand. As you'd imagine, future selves' faces went from appearing sad to appearing happy as people directed increasing amounts of money toward retirement; images of their present selves behaved oppositely. Here again, those who could see the emotional expressions of their future selves decided to save more for retirement than did those who saw only their present selves precisely because it was now easier to feel compassion for what had heretofore only been an abstraction. Virtual reality allowed the distress a future self might feel to be visualized in much the same way it would appear on the face of an actual person.

Compassion, not rational planning or willpower, doubled the savings rate. It produced an effortless self-control where before the id primarily ruled. This might seem somewhat surprising, but it makes great sense to people who, in many ways, are the world's masters of delayed gratification: Buddhist monks.

THE MORALITY OF MEDITATION

If you want to truly understand something, it often pays to go right to the top. By virtue of their experience, people who sit at the pinnacle of a field usually hold a sweeping, authoritative, and even esoteric perspective on how things work. They've seen it all before, been in the trenches, and emerged with wisdom few others have attained. So when it comes to self-control, Buddhist monks, who daily benefit from millennia of teachings and thought on the perils of giving in to craving and selfish temptations, have a lot to say.

In Buddhism, the word *tanha,* which roughly translates to craving or desire, explicitly refers to a motive to grasp and maintain pleasurable experiences or, conversely, to avoid painful or unpleasant ones. In essence, *tanha* is a craving for enjoyment in the here and now, future consequences be damned. *Tanha* is also identified as a root cause of what the Buddhists term *dukkha:* suffering, anxiety, and general unhappiness. For adherents of this faith, self-centered desires for pleasure are a form of ignorance that gets in the way of well-being and the ultimate goal of enlightenment. Selfless actions, which include improving one's own ethics as well as aiding others, build karma points. And those points, according to Buddhist beliefs, enable a person's successive reincarnation to come closer to ultimate liberation. Now, that's an intertemporal framework if there ever was one!

Whether or not you accept the religious aspects of Buddhist teachings isn't relevant for our purposes here. What is relevant is that over thousands of years, Buddhist scholars have built up their own understanding of the workings of the mind — an understanding that has many parallels to the secrets being unlocked by the modern sciences of psychology and neurology. Combine this with the special emphasis Buddhist teachers have placed on developing meditation techniques for squelching harmful desires, and it's clear that they might be able to offer some deep insights into self-control and perseverance.

In 2015 I had the good fortune to have several discussions with internationally renowned Buddhist teacher Trungram Gyaltrul Rinpoche in which I broached this topic. Rinpoche occupies a unique position in the Buddhist world. Not only is he recognized as one of the highest *tulkus* (reincarnated teachers) of the Kagyu school of Tibetan Buddhism, but he is also the first Tibetan lama to complete a PhD at Harvard. As such, he straddles the East-West intellectual divide in a way few others can.

When I asked Rinpoche about self-control and avoiding temptations, our conversation naturally drifted toward meditation. I expected we'd discuss it as a tool to increase concentration and, thereby, willpower. On the off chance you haven't noticed, mindfulness has been all the rage. A quick perusal of articles from the *New York Times,* the *Atlantic,* and other popular media provides ample evidence that meditation leads to all kinds of great cognitive outcomes. It'll increase your scores on standardized tests, enhance your creativity, and even make you more productive at work. In short, it's touted as a kind of "supercharger" for the mind. These claims are justified because much of meditation training focuses on learning how to master attention, thought flow, and focus, all of which are closely related to executive function. And since such cognitive abilities can be used for self-control, the notion that meditation lessens cravings and increases success seems to logically follow. So imagine my happy surprise when Rinpoche told me that all the cognitive benefits of meditation — better focus, better memory, et cetera — were traditionally considered secondary to its true purpose: development of a deep and abiding compassion. All the cognitive training is simply a means to an end, and it is that end — a feeling of great compassion for all beings — that ultimately makes self-control and related virtues more automatic.

The central role played by compassion is often ignored, thanks to a historical accident. The scientists who first began to study meditation were primarily neuroscientists and those interested in cognition and memory. The questions they asked about meditation were guided by their own interests: What does it do to and for the brain? The result was a decade's worth of findings showing that meditation enhances cognitive skills. But if you think about it from a historical standpoint, the goals of early meditation teachers such as Gautama Buddha weren't enhancing test scores or memory. To the contrary, they were centered on fostering ethical decisions and compassionate behavior, or as the Buddhists say, on ending suffering. But because these phenomena were inherently social in nature, they were ignored as neuroscientists turned their lenses on what meditation could do to enhance the information-processing power of the brain. This was a gap I wanted to fill. If meditation, compassion, and self-control were truly linked, as Buddhist philosophy posits, we first needed to find some evidence, and that required studying the effects of meditation in an entirely new way.

The first step in most scientific investigations of meditation is to recruit people who aren't Buddhists and who haven't previously practiced meditation. To do that, we placed ads in and around Boston inviting people to take part in an eight-week meditation study for which they would be paid. The only requirement was that they be true novices; they couldn't have had any previous training. Once we had a list of volunteers, we randomly assigned half to complete eight weeks of meditation training. Since we also needed a comparison group, we told the remaining volunteers that they were on a waitlist. To make sure the training was authentic, we enlisted the help of master teacher Lama Willa Miller, who met regularly with participants to offer instruction and guidance in meditation practice. And to ensure people were continuing to practice correctly when not in her class, Miller also gave them audio recordings she created to use at home.

We now had two groups of people who were equally interested in meditation, but only one of which contained people who actually had some degree of authentic training. This is the point where most scientists would serve up a memory or attention test for their participants, or scan their brains in search of changes in white-matter density. Not us, although that's not exactly what we told our participants. They believed that at the end of the eight weeks they'd be coming to the lab to have their cognitive skills tested. Little did they know that the true experiment would begin in the waiting room.

If we wanted to examine meditation's effects on compassion and self-control, we needed to do it in a fairly normal environment. One that, unlike most MRI tubes, had more than one real person inside it. In short, we needed to design a challenge that would offer people the opportunity to keep a mild comfort or to give it up to benefit someone in pain. After considering many options, we landed on a situation that was as familiar in its dynamics as it was theoretically elegant in its explanatory power. When our participants arrived in the lab's waiting room, they saw three chairs. The first two were occupied by actors working for us. So, as you'd expect, each participant (as they were scheduled to come to the lab one at a time) would sit down in the remaining chair to await being called into the lab for testing. After a few minutes had passed, the relative quiet of the waiting room was interrupted by an elevator door sliding open at the opposite end of the hall. Out came a young woman on crutches who had her foot in an orthopedic boot. The woman, who also worked for us, hobbled down the hall, wincing a bit with each step, until she entered the waiting room, where, somewhat dejectedly, she leaned against the wall with a bit of a whimper, as every chair was taken.

What would participants do? If they wanted to act nobly, the answer was clear: offer her their chair. But that meant sacrificing their own immediate comfort to aid another and thus would take some degree of self-control. That might sound like an overstatement on my part, as many people might (and did when we asked them) predict that a solid majority of people placed in this position would have readily offered up their chair. As it turned out, though, only 16 percent of "normal" people in our experiment — and by normal I mean the ones who hadn't meditated for the previous eight weeks — suggested that the woman in pain take their seat.

This was a dispiriting finding, and sadly it wasn't a fluke. We ran the experiment a second time and got similar results. Now, truth be told, we were stacking the deck a little. The other people who were sitting in the room when a participant arrived — the actors who didn't offer their chairs — had been instructed by us to ignore the woman on crutches. They were to read a book or thumb their phones as she entered, appearing to pay her no heed. Yet the sighs and similar sounds of discomfort she uttered were audible enough for everyone to hear, meaning it was clear to our participants that these others were willfully feigning ignorance of the injured woman's plight. That was the point. This type of mass indifference is specially meant to reduce people's motivations to help. If nobody else is bothering to assist someone in need, why should you? It's a pernicious phenomenon known as the bystander effect, and it allows people to stand by passively while all manner of suffering occurs right in front of them. In our experiments it worked all too well.

When we examined the meditators, however, quite a different story emerged. After only eight weeks of mindfulness practice, the percentage of people who felt compassion and sacrificed their own comfort to aid the woman in pain more than tripled, rising to 50 percent. That's a big difference, and one we and others have been able to replicate using related measures of compassionate behavior. When considered in combination, these findings show how meditation bolsters self-control via compassion. They make clear, in essence, that Rinpoche was right. As I noted at this book's outset, people often need self-control to act with kindness and generosity. Whether that self-control is aimed at sacrificing to aid others or their own future selves, they need a push to give up their immediate comfort and thereby raise the likelihood that they'll benefit from a returned favor or a better outcome down the line. And while it's true that we can remind ourselves daily to be kind and exert the requisite willpower to behave accordingly, practicing mindfulness —a route by which compassion begins to emerge automatically and continuously— offers a better route.

BUDDHA BRAIN

To Buddhist teachers such as Rinpoche, the results of these experiments were nothing new. They have seen compassion grow with meditation practice time and again, and to degrees much greater than what my team could demonstrate in two months. But to me, the findings transformed an article of faith into a scientific fact, and in so doing gave me even greater respect for the insights meditation masters have to offer about how the human mind works. In truth, I continue to be struck by how closely some Buddhist views parallel the arguments I was making based on modern psychological science. For example, when thinking of a Buddhist monk, people commonly envision a person who resembles *Star Trek's* Mr. Spock: logical but emotionless. That is, we expect a monk's mastery of cravings to stem from a negation of their emotional lives. If they can control their emotions, they don't have to feel them. And if they don't feel them, they won't be tempted by desire. In reality, though, this view captures only half the picture.

When monks begin training, they take vows. They swear to abstain from lying, alcohol, stealing, harming others, and sexual misconduct. In essence, they agree to avoid behaviors that offer immediate pleasure but future ruin. Early on in their practice, keeping these vows is often difficult. Like the modern student trying to study for an exam or the gambler trying to resist reaching for his ATM card, the monks attempt to rely on willpower and motivated reasoning to succeed. For example, novice monks might refrain from drinking not because they truly don't want to imbibe — they probably do — but because they desire respect from their superiors. They want their teachers and peers to see them as a success, so they struggle mightily to avoid giving in to temptation. But the result is frequent failure. Sometimes willpower crumbles. Other times, if they think they can get away with it without anyone knowing, they will down an intoxicating beverage. Like the participants in my experiments on cheating, the monks can convince themselves that it's okay to break the rules and, therefore, not learn from their mistakes. Self-control, at this stage, tends to be unstable.

As training progresses, however, monks spend more time in select meditation practices, one goal of which is to sharpen their awareness and, thereby, gain control of their emotions. Daily life for many of us consists of a constant stream of changing feelings. One minute we're feeling happy while sharing doughnuts with a coworker; the next minute we're angry about a slight from a manager; the next, we're nervous that we might be late for a meeting, and then sympathetic toward (and perhaps even a bit disgusted by) a homeless person we pass on the way to lunch. As they're meant to do, these vacillating emotions constantly update and alter our minds' calculations about what to decide and how to act. Feel angry and you're more likely to lash out at someone. Feel disgusted and you're more likely to avoid him. This reality led the Buddhist masters to realize that a first step in overcoming temptation is to exert some control on the mind's computations. Leaving them to be altered willy-nilly by seemingly random emotions, while potentially adaptive in the moment, doesn't guarantee progress toward long-term success. And so, as part of meditation practice, monks learn to filter what they attend to and how they perceive things. In doing so, they gradually gain the ability to reduce the turbulent emotions evoked by their surroundings.

These initial steps do indeed conform to what most people expect of a monk's emotional life: the calming and control of feelings. They also match the current perspective on how to achieve self-control: use cognitive mechanisms to let emotions pass and thus reduce their impact on the mind. But the story doesn't end there. For Buddhists, emotions aren't inherently good or bad; they're a form of mental energy. And like any powerful force, they can be constructive or destructive depending on how they're harnessed. Later phases of meditative training involve a rekindling of emotion. But it's a reawakening in which one is no longer a slave to but rather master of one's feelings. The initial steps that involve learning how to quiet and control feelings make way for later ones centered on transforming emotions. Here monks learn to use feelings as tools to achieve their goals, with compassion being a primary force.

This compassion fundamentally alters how self-control works. Where before monks had to rely on the tenuous strength of willpower and rational analysis to keep their vows, now the cravings that tempted them seem to vanish. Compassion, like gratitude, decreases the value we attach to objects and events that offer immediate gratification and thus makes it easier to persevere in ways that pay off in the future. For Buddhist monks, the ultimate goal is the end of all creatures' suffering. As you may remember, pursuing this goal has led to actions of great self-sacrifice by some, even of their own lives through self-immolation when they believed this action could end violence against others. Rinpoche himself dropped everything to spend months organizing and participating in difficult relief missions in Nepal following devastating earthquakes in 2015. If that's not true grit, I'm not sure what is.

I should repeat here that my goal in discussing Buddhist views on compassion and self-control isn't to convert people to that religion. Likewise, I'm not saying that everyone's long-term goal should be the end of all suffering. I am saying that the insights offered by a tradition that has studied self-control for thousands of years should be taken seriously, especially when they begin to dovetail with recent scientific findings, as does the Buddhist notion that self-control is best enhanced not by stifling emotions but by using ones such as compassion to foster it.

Still, for all the parallels in these two approaches, we have yet to see firm evidence that it was feelings of compassion that drove self-control. Yes, we've seen that meditation increases compassion and self-restraint, but it is possible that, despite Buddhist theology, there's something else about meditation — something besides compassion — that was working to enhance self-control. After all, meditation benefits both cognitive and emotional mechanisms. Let me offer an example proving that compassion — by itself and irrespective of its source — boosts self-restraint when it's needed.

PEACE BE WITH YOU

Until now, I've tended to focus on aspects of self-control that relate to performance and abilities: persevering in the face of difficulty, working or studying long hours, saving money for the future, and the like. But there's another area in which self-control is paramount:

aggression. When hostility is imminent, you're likely to hear people urging others to "calm down" or to "control yourself." In short, they're admonishing people to tamp down their anger lest it lead to regret. Aggression of any type can leave lasting scars. While in the moment it might feel really good, even empowering, to dominate or punish someone, doing so repeatedly leads to adverse consequences.

Anger and aggression must serve some purpose, though, given how commonly we see them. And in truth, they do. Intimidation and violence can be an effective way to achieve goals, especially in the short run. Sometimes combat or brute force is a necessary evil. Without the ability to fight back when the stakes for survival are high, we would be at a disadvantage against others who threaten us. As a result, humans, like many other animals, come equipped with a capacity to aggress in order to achieve our goals. Unfortunately, the instances in which some are willing to use aggression aren't always appropriate, and as we'll soon see, habitual aggression and antisocial behavior are a recipe for long-term disaster.

Although there are several modern theories of aggression, with most agreeing on a few basic facts, the I³ model developed by Northwestern University psychologist Eli Finkel offers the most authoritative and efficient account. The name I³ comes from the three facets, or phases, of an aggressive response: instigation, impellance, and inhibition. Instigation refers to the triggering phase. There has to be something in a given situation — an insult, a frustration, an injury — that makes someone feel angry. No one is constantly aggressive; something has to set them off. Of course, the trigger that sets aggression in motion doesn't actually have to be related to the eventual target. People can, and often do, take out their frustrations on third parties who are "safer" and thus less likely to fight back. For example, when annoyed by the boss, people often pick on a subordinate, paying it forward in an evil sort of way.

Not everyone reacts to a potential trigger in the same way, however. Nor does the same trigger always make the same person aggressive. One reason for this has to do with the idea of impellance: some force must push a person toward hostile behavior. Like triggers, impelling forces come in many types, from biological ones such as increased testosterone levels to situational ones such as physical pain or exposure to violent media. Depending on the mix of factors, the odds that any one of us might act in a way we'll come to regret can go up or down. But it's the third and final phase of the I³ model that I want to focus on here — the phase where the brakes can be applied. In this inhibition phase, our minds have one last opportunity to prevent aggressive impulses from determining what we do. One of the primary brakes is, of course, executive function. Yet, if the ability to tamp down aggression through willpower wanes, whether due to alcohol, fatigue, or even biased reasoning that attempts to justify a violent act, the floodgates remain open, letting the triggered hostility flow unimpeded.

Although there are many lab-based examples of this phenomenon — for example, people with impaired frontal lobes (where executive function resides) give stronger electric shocks to those who provoke them — one of my favorite pieces of supporting evidence comes from Finkel's examination of a vast trove of data collected on Americans between February 2001 and April 2003. Researchers from the University of Michigan conducted face-to-face interviews with thousands of people across the United States, collecting, among many other pieces of information, data on the frequency of violence committed toward intimate partners (for example, pushing, shoving, slapping, threatening), tendencies toward having an explosive personality, and chronic feelings of being mentally drained or "worn out" (which translates to a lessened ability for executive function).

Unsurprisingly, the findings showed that an explosive personality predicted increased violence toward intimate partners. But so, too, did feelings of being mentally drained. What's more, this effect held even when accounting for factors such as feeling stressed, depressed, and the like, indicating that an inability to exert executive function was a direct predictor of violence. The most toxic effects for aggression, though, stemmed from a combination of disposition and reduced executive function — people who were volatile and lacking in self-control. When the floodgates opened for these folks, a tidal wave of hostility rushed out.

These and many related findings show that when something in one's environs triggers an aggressive impulse, anyone whose executive function is inhibited for any reason can act in ways that are unethical and destructive to their future goals and happiness. And for the hotheaded among us, the problem is magnified. Here again we can see the potential for cognitive strategies to fail, which raises the question of whether, as was the case with gratitude, an emotion-based strategy might prove more reliable in restraining potentially harmful behavior. Such a strategy would entail not repressing destructive emotions but replacing, or as the Buddhists might say, transforming them into virtuous ones.

When my colleague Paul Condon and I decided to examine this issue, we realized that we first had to solve a problem: we needed a way to get people angry within the context of our lab. Put in I³ terminology, we needed an instigating event. As it turned out, a method wasn't too difficult to find. Francesca Gino, a professor at Harvard Business School, along with behavioral economist Dan Ariely, had developed a ruse that induced people to cheat.

The procedure worked by putting people in a room and telling them that they had five minutes to complete a set of easy math problems. The more problems anyone solved, the more money they would get. Sounds simple enough, but Gino and Ariely weren't telling their participants the whole story. One of the people in the room was an actor whose role was to cheat. After a few minutes had passed in which everyone seemed to be working away, he would stand up and announce that he had completed all the problems — an achievement everyone knew was clearly impossible given the time allowed. But as the instructions were for people to drop their anonymous worksheets into a recycling box before taking money corresponding to the number of problems they'd completed, the actor could take his unearned cash without fear of his treachery being unmasked. In theory, it would be impossible for anyone to confirm exactly how many problems he finished.

Of course, Gino and Ariely didn't tell participants that each person's worksheet was marked with a secret code that later allowed them to compare the true number of problems completed with the number reported, for which participants paid themselves. As they anticipated, the simple act of witnessing someone cheat on the task increased the likelihood that others would follow suit. After all, why not? If cheating allowed that guy to take more money, then cheating in the same way should work for anyone else, too. Once again we see that logic and reason don't always lead to better self-control.

In our case, we didn't need people to cheat, we needed them to aggress. So we took advantage of the basic human desire to punish transgressors by making two minor tweaks to the setup. First, we rigged it so that our participants would always have to report how many problems they finished before they saw the actor cheat. On average, people completed about five of the twenty problems. And as no one had cheated yet, and their peers could observe their behavior, people tended to be pretty honest in reporting their success accurately. Right before it was time for the last person — the actor — to tell the experimenter how many problems he had completed, the experimenter, by design, stepped briefly out of the room to get more cash. As soon as he was gone, the actor got up and placed his worksheets into a shredder — which we used instead of a recycling box to ensure there was no paper trail — and then waited for the experimenter to return. When he did, the actor smugly reported that he had finished all twenty problems and, because he wanted to save the experimenter time, had already placed his worksheets in the shredder. He had previously seen the experimenter tell the other participants to place their worksheets in the shredder after they reported their scores, so this statement was believable. Everyone, including the slightly stunned-looking experimenter, knew that finishing all twenty problems was next to impossible. Yet, without proof that the actor was lying — the evidence was shredded — the experimenter had no recourse but to let him take the unearned money. And given that the actor was the last in the room to report his scores, it was too late for any of our regular participants to follow suit. All they could do was seethe.

Before everyone left, however, there was one more task to complete: one that purportedly involved taste perception. Here our participants were given the opportunity to prepare taste samples for one another. It was a simple job: pour liquid out of a bottle into a small sample cup. Whatever was poured into that cup would be placed, in its entirety, into the mouth of another participant in order, who would rate it as a test of gustatory acuity. By design, all participants thought they were selected to prepare the taste sample for the guy who had just cheated and with whom they were understandably quite angry. And as luck would have it (well, really there was no luck involved at all), the liquid they were to pour into the sample cup would be used to assess the actor's perceptions of spiciness. There in front of them was a bottle of wicked-looking hot sauce with a corresponding warning label about its high Scoville, or heat, level.

With this ruse, we had just offered our participants an avenue for aggression. They knew that ingesting the hot sauce would be quite painful and that whatever amount they put into the sample cup would be placed into the cheater's mouth in its entirety. It was a diabolical equation: more hot sauce in the sample cup equals more pain to the cheater. Under normal conditions—where people are making samples for others whom they hadn't seen cheat—they pour sparingly. The average amount is about two grams. But when they poured for the cheater, they quadrupled it. They wanted the guy to suffer. It goes without saying that we didn't actually make him ingest it, but our participants didn't know that as they were pouring the liquid pain.

At this point we had our anger and our aggression. All we needed now was a way to transform that anger into compassion. While contemplative training might make this an automatic process, we wanted to evoke compassion in a different way this time. So we decided to use a little sleight of hand by running the experiment again but with one final twist. In this version there were two actors: the one who cheated as before and a new one, whose purpose was to induce compassion in others.

Fortunately for us, this new confederate was a fantastic actress. As the first actor was cheating, she surreptitiously placed saline drops in her eyes while true participants were distracted watching him. Then she began to sniffle. And then break into a soft cry. At that point, the experimenter would go over to her to ask if she was okay, at which point she'd say, "No . . . I found out a few days ago that my brother has cancer. I'm sorry for breaking down . . . I'm not going to be able to go home to see him until this weekend, but it's really upsetting me right now." At that point the experimenter excused her. Witnessing this scene evoked feelings of sympathy and compassion from our participants—a fact that we could objectively see when we measured their emotional responses. Following this brief interruption, the experiment proceeded as usual with the opportunity to punish the cheater up next.

What happened was rather astounding. People were still quite angry at the guy who cheated — angry in the sense that they believed what he did was wrong — but they stopped themselves from harming him. The amount of hot sauce they poured was indistinguishable from what was poured when he didn't cheat. Simply put, their aggression had vanished. They did not become timid or ambivalent. They were more than willing to condemn his actions and express a desire to have him correct it. It's just that their desire — their impelling force — to lash out at him was gone. As a result, they didn't have to rely on the tenuous power of executive function to overrule an aggressive impulse. An upwelling of compassion, even though it was directed at someone else, was enough to prevent an escalation of violence, thereby working to benefit the future.

This view — that reducing aggression benefited the future — warrants a bit more explanation. As I noted earlier, aggression can be useful in certain instances, but in situations where it isn't needed for immediate self-protection, like this one, it's usually not. Here, the cheating was done. What purpose would aggression serve? While humans do sometimes engage in what's called *third-party punishment* — punishing people who have wronged others in order to reinforce social norms — doing so via aggression isn't always the best strategy. For one, it has the potential to escalate conflict. Although it might feel good to punish someone today, there's always the chance that this decision will backfire tomorrow. If the target of hostility doesn't acknowledge and accept the error of his ways, a spiral of increasing tit-for-tat aggressive acts can ensue.

There's another reason, though, why aggression doesn't benefit the future — ours or anyone else's. Work by Harvard's Martin Nowak shows that adopting an aggressive, punishing nature not only limits people's success over the long run but also limits that of the groups to which they belong. Nowak and his colleagues conducted a series of experiments where people played multiple rounds of a computer game in which they would be randomly paired with others. That meant that over time they would come into contact with specific others more than once. In each round of the game, people could choose to cooperate, cheat, or punish their partner. Cooperation meant sacrificing some initial money for a larger future payoff if a partner also cooperated. For example, each player would put $1 into the pot, and if both chose to cooperate, each would get $2 back. Cheating meant not contributing to the pot, or in essence taking $1 at the expense of your partner. So, if both cheated, there would be no profit. Finally, punishment meant choosing to pay $1 to have $4 taken away from your partner if he cheated.

After observing hundreds of rounds of the game, Nowak's team found that although aggressive punishment for past misdeeds could increase cooperation, the best outcomes (that is, the most money), both for individuals and for their groups, occurred in the absence of such aggressive acts. Here again we see that what strategy leads to success depends on the time horizon we're considering. In the short term, aggression can surely force people to change their ways and be fair or cooperate, but it also festers, causing further cycles of violence that diminish everyone's success over time. Using self-control to refrain from hostile behavior does the opposite. The people and groups who were most successful over time didn't aggress. The winners didn't punish and, as a result, averaged double the profit of those who regularly did. Now, it's important to realize that this doesn't mean that winners were suckers. They can and should still reinforce ethical behavior in others through nonviolent means, but the ability to act with self-restraint — to not aggress toward others but rather desire to help them learn the error of their ways — pays the most dividends over time.

To close the circle that I began here with meditation's influence on compassion, it's useful to note that meditation increases compassion not simply toward strangers but even toward people who would normally evoke aggression. In some of our most recent work, people who had completed several weeks of meditation practice were significantly less likely to seek revenge against others who had insulted them. And in support of the view I'm advocating here, this reduction in aggression toward provocateurs wasn't associated with any differences in executive function — a factor we assessed as part of the study — but rather stemmed from a simple increase in compassion.

In findings like these, we can glimpse the convergence of virtue and evolutionary adaptation I mentioned earlier when it comes to compassion and other socially oriented emotions. I'm saying not that science should try to support religious dogma but rather that some spiritual principles may be based on an intuition of what's truly beneficial for human flourishing. In the case of compassion, I think this is particularly true.

FORGIVE, FORGET, AND FLOURISH

If compassion only helped us inhibit poor treatment of others, I'd probably not be spending much time on it in this book. But like gratitude and pride, that's not the case. What ties these three emotions together is that their ability to make us willing to sacrifice to aid others can be coopted to help our future selves.

For many, teaching perseverance — the ability to keep working hard to achieve a goal — means "tiger momming" themselves or their kids. They critically rehash failures in an attempt to make themselves or others work harder the next time. But our work on compassion suggests that there might be another way to go — using compassion while acknowledging failures with a sense of warmth and forgiveness. While many might initially think that this sensitive approach could lead to complacency and subsequent reduced effort, it turns out that the compassionate route is the better way to go. Feeling compassion doesn't mean accepting poor performance; it doesn't make people blind to failure. To the contrary, when we feel compassion, whether for ourselves or others, it makes us want to help them do better, become better, but without causing any additional pain. Remember, it's not that the people in my experiment on cheating and compassion believed that the cheater was now an okay guy or that he shouldn't alter his behavior; it's just that they didn't want to make him change his behavior through aggression or hostility. Compassion should work the same way when it's directed at oneself. It should acknowledge failure, while motivating a desire to sacrifice enjoyment in the moment in order to improve the future but without punishing or belittling oneself.

We can see this principle in action through research by Berkeley psychologists Juliana Breines and Serena Chen. The duo recruited more than one hundred students for a study on standardized test performance and sat them down to complete two sets of problems taken from the verbal portion of the Graduate Record Examination (GRE). After the students had finished the first set, Breines and Chen handed out an answer key and allowed participants to score their own exam. As the problems were particularly difficult, the average score was only 40 percent. Nobody was pleased with their result; everyone wanted to do better in the next round. Breines and Chen then offered study materials to the students so that any who wished could use them to improve their performance on the second set of GRE problems.

At this point — right before any studying could begin — compassion came into play. One-third of the students received a message that it was common for people to have difficulty with tests like the one they had just taken, and thus they shouldn't be too hard on themselves. They should treat themselves with compassion, not criticism, in response to their previous test performance. Another third were told that they shouldn't feel badly about themselves because they were actually intelligent, as proven by their having gotten in to Berkeley. And the final third were told nothing at all.

The students who were encouraged to treat their initial subpar performance with understanding and forgiveness subsequently increased the time they spent studying by 30 percent, compared with students in the other two groups. And in this experiment, as in life, the additional time spent studying was a strong predictor of performance on the next exam. It also wasn't the case that self-compassion led students to believe that they would perform better; their predictions for success on the second exam weren't any higher than those of students in the other groups. Rather, feelings of compassion made them more willing to accept the costs of studying in the moment in the hopes that their future rewards would be worth it.

Compassion has similar effects on procrastination. A study involving more than two hundred college students revealed a strong link between compassion toward oneself and progress toward academic goals. Students who typically had lower levels of self-compassion procrastinated more and, as one might expect, had poorer academic outcomes.

Increased perseverance due to self-compassion can also be seen among athletes. Those who more regularly report forgiving and empathizing with themselves for failures, as opposed to criticizing themselves, show greater initiative when it comes to future practice. A similar pattern holds even among non-athletes; those who tend to treat themselves with compassion typically show a greater motivation to exercise. In fact, when it comes to engaging in most any healthy behavior, the story is much the same. For example, smokers who report higher levels of self-compassion succeed more often when trying to quit. Compassion, whether we consciously realize it or not, nudges us toward many types of decisions and behaviors that help us in the future.

As with gratitude, it's also important to recognize that compassion can heal the body. Unlike straining to use willpower, it buffers body and mind against the havoc caused by stress and anxiety. The initial symptoms of stress — the ones we feel when we're suddenly under pressure — are quite familiar: accelerating heart rate, feelings of constriction in the chest, a tightness in the voice, and a stomach in knots. All of these are controlled to some degree by the vagus nerve, which, when firing, calms all these aspects of the stress response. You can think of the vagus as a brake. The more it's activated, the more relaxed you feel; it slows the heart, relaxes abdominal muscles, and loosens the larynx. Its activity signals your body that the environment is safe and, thus, is one in which you can focus on whatever interests you. There's no emergency, meaning you have time to be creative and to pursue goals beyond immediate survival.

Given the vagus's function, any psychological state that enhances its activity — or vagal tone, as it's usually termed — should guard against stress. And work by University of Toronto psychologist Jennifer Stellar on compassion shows just that. Stellar was among the first to show a strong link between compassion and vagal tone. When she induced people to feel compassion by exposing them to others who needed help, the amount of compassion they felt was directly tied to vagal activity: those who felt more compassion showed elevated vagal tone.

This link between compassion and vagal tone suggests that people who regularly cultivate this emotion should experience some resilience in the face of stress. And indeed, that appears to be the case. Research by University of North Carolina psychologist Karen Bluth found that a tendency toward self-compassion strongly predicted both a lowered stress response and a greater sense of well-being. When she subjected her participants to the Trier social stress test — the one in which people have to give a presentation in front of stonefaced evaluators — those who more frequently forgave themselves for perceived stumbles and engaged in less self-criticism experienced less stress as measured by their cardiac and hormonal responses during the presentation. Regularly feeling compassion, then, heals the body while it enables the mind to strive to meet its goals.

GAMING THE SYSTEM

Although the benefits of compassion are many, the ways to cultivate it aren't obvious. Unlike gratitude, it's not as simple as regularly counting blessings. People could watch a documentary about suffering in different parts of the world, but that would also likely lead to feelings of depression or sadness. What's more, most of us would quickly habituate to such scenes.

As I showed at the start of this chapter, meditation offers one route to growing compassion. But it's a route characterized by many potential bumps. Not everyone has easy access to a skilled teacher, and even among those who do, time constraints and financial limitations can make it a difficult training regimen to follow. Luckily, though, we're living in an age where there's an easy way to deal with such challenges: mobile tech. Using a meditation app might sound silly at first, but it turns out that if you choose the right one — one whose methods were developed by a person with substantial training — you can get similar benefits to those coming from face-to-face instruction.

To demonstrate this fact, we partnered with Andy Puddicombe at Headspace — the company that makes the Headspace mindfulness app — in an attempt to replicate our earlier findings showing that meditation leads to compassion. Puddicombe, who spent years studying meditation in a Buddhist monastery, designed the app to incorporate well-established training techniques. As such, it's about as close as you can get to studying with a master teacher while being able to practice your skills in your living room or on the train to work. After letting half of our participants use Headspace for three weeks, as opposed to a similar app that focused on enhancing executive function, we brought all of them back to that same waiting room and confronted them, one by one, with the woman-on-crutches scenario. Once again, those who meditated showed increased compassion for the "sufferer"; 37 percent of them got up to offer her their chair, while only the usual 14 percent of non-meditators did. That 23 percent increase in acting compassionately wasn't quite as large as what we found in our first study, but then again, we only had people practicing meditation for half as long. This experiment does show that compassion can be quite easily cultivated using a smartphone app for ten to fifteen minutes a day. And given compassion's ties to increased self-control and perseverance, any extra ten to fifteen minutes you might have will be better spent practicing mindfulness than trying to boost your executive function with so-called brain building apps like the one we used in our control condition.

For all its benefits, though, meditation isn't for everyone. And, in truth, not everyone needs it. Millions of compassionate people have never closed their eyes while sitting cross-legged on a cushion. So it should come as no surprise that there are other ways to encourage our minds to take up compassion. One of the most promising works via a simple exercise: find a link — any link — with others.

Whether we realize it or not, the human mind attempts to categorize everyone we meet based on a multitude of labels: race, gender, class, religion, hometown, et cetera. At any given moment, one of these categories is salient, and that's the biased lens through which we view someone. By biased, I mean that in determining how similar any given person is to us (that is, same religion, from the same hometown), our minds alter how willing we are to help that person in a time of need. At both a psychological and biological level, a bias toward favoring similar others makes good sense: the costs associated with feeling and easing the pain of people who are close to us are more worthwhile, as they're the people who are most likely to return the favor down the line. This is exactly how many immigrant groups function when they move to new countries. They live together in enclaves and support one another during hard times, often in a very insular way.

Given that acting compassionately toward others is an intertemporal decision — providing resources for them now with a hope (even an unconscious one), but no guarantee, for reciprocation in the future — it only makes sense in an evolutionary perspective if the odds of the other returning the favor are decent. Hence the focus on similarity. Helping out a member of one's team — however *team* is defined — makes receiving payback more likely, as the goals of both people are aligned. Put simply, it's a safer bet to act compassionately toward others with whom you share reciprocal investments; they're less likely to take the favor and run. These calculations are not usually conscious, but they do occur. And they run very, very deep. So deep that they can influence not only the compassion you feel toward people you've long known but even the compassion you feel for those you've just met.

To show just how deeply rooted this bias is, Piercarlo Valdesolo and I decided to focus on the most seemingly insignificant marker of affiliation we could find: motor synchrony. It's exactly what it sounds like: moving parts of two bodies in time. We thought it would work, as perceiving objects of any kind to move in unison is normally interpreted to mean that they're joined in some way — two pieces of a greater whole. What's more, synchrony offered the benefit of being untethered to any preexisting social categories, enabling us to create a sense of similarity from thin air.

To accomplish this, we brought people into our lab for what they thought was an experiment about music perception. When they arrived, we sat them across a table from an actor who they believed was just another participant. We had them put on headphones and then simply tap their hand on the sensor placed in front of them whenever they heard a tone. The actor did the same. The trick was that we rigged the tones so that some people would hear the same sounds as the actor, resulting in the pair tapping their hands in unison with each other. For others, we set the tones to occur completely at random, meaning that there was no matching of tapping motions at all.

After the tapping, during which no words were spoken, we separated the two and asked our participants how similar they thought they were to the person who had been sitting across from them. Next, through a bit of stagecraft, they witnessed the actor get cheated by another person during a task-assignment procedure, resulting in him getting unfairly stuck having to complete more onerous work in the lab than anyone else. People were then able to note how much compassion they felt for his plight and could, if they wished, volunteer to take on some of the actor's workload.

The simple act of having tapped hands in time with another person made our participants believe they were more similar to him. They weren't quite sure why, but they nonetheless felt some sort of link with him. As we had expected, synchronized movement served as a marker of similarity. This phenomenon isn't really that surprising. We see it in ritual. We see it in military marching. We see it in team-building dances, like the Maori haka. It's a message to the brain that right here, right now, people's goals and outcomes are joined. And so our participants tried to create stories to explain the feelings of similarity their minds had already generated. Some believed the actor was in their freshman English class; others thought he had been a guest at a large party they'd attended the previous week. None of these were true. Nonetheless, that increased sense of similarity made people feel more compassion for his plight. Even though he was always victimized by the cheater in the same way, those who felt more affiliated with him due to having tapped in synch were willing to feel his pain more than were those who didn't share any sense of similarity. That boost in compassion also translated into a greater willingness to help him by volunteering to take on some of his workload.

On one hand, these findings show the unfortunate, socially bounded nature of compassion. Like it or not, there's a parochial bias in when and how we feel it. But on the upside, they also suggest a way to grow compassion that centers not on fighting the system but on gaming it. If feelings of similarity enhance compassion, and something as simple as tapping your hands produces a noticeable difference, then all you really need to do to start feeling more compassion is to start changing the ways you think about others. There's nothing magical about tapping. Any cue of similarity will do. We've repeated the experiment by having people wear the same color wristbands and found the same results. When viewed together, these findings suggest that simply taking the time to look for and think about what you have in common with others is a surefire way to feel more compassion for them if and when it's needed.

For example, in Boston, where I live, using this strategy might mean trying not to think about your new neighbor as the guy from New York who likes the dreaded Yankees but rather as a fan of the local coffee shop that you also like. Or thinking about the person sitting across from you on the bus not as someone of a different ethnic group but as a fellow denizen of your city. Looking for commonalities, as opposed to emphasizing differences, will go a long way to increasing your tendency to care about the welfare of others, allowing you to experience an emotion that buttresses your own self-control.

I recognize that this recommendation might sound trite. So let me offer one of my favorite examples to show just how powerful emphasizing similarity can be. In December of 1914, outside of Ypres, Belgium, the British and the Germans had been facing off in a bloody battle. On Christmas Eve, as the Brits sat in their trenches staring across the field that divided them from their German adversaries, they began to hear singing. Then they saw flickers of light. Although most weren't fluent enough in German to translate the lyrics, the tunes were all familiar. The Germans were singing Christmas carols and lighting candles. Some of the British then took the extraordinary step of signaling and then approaching the men who hours before had been trying to kill them. The Germans acted in kind. What unfolded next has come to be known as the Christmas Eve truce. The men began to talk, share pictures of their families, and even exchange presents.

A central reason for this surprising event can be traced to the songs themselves. In those moments when the British and Germans realized that they were about to celebrate the same religious holiday, they came to see the social identity they shared. They viewed one another not in terms of nationality but in terms of religion. They were no longer Germans and British but fellow Christians. They no longer wanted to harm one another but rather felt empathy. And while uncommon, this event certainly isn't unique. In 2006, factions who had been battling each other in the Ivory Coast for several years put down their weapons and celebrated together in peace as the national team qualified for the World Cup. Here again, people who had been fighting one another were suddenly brought together through emphasizing a joint identity as opposed to factional ones.

I admit that these examples represent extreme cases. But in their extremity, they suggest what can be achieved by seeking similarity. If similarity can at times make people willing to trust and empathize with others who a day before were trying to shoot them, it should be able more frequently to foster a lesser sacrifice meant to aid another. When combined with our work demonstrating the power that identifying a small and even trivial association can exert on compassion and its resulting prosocial behaviors, pausing daily to take the time to look for links with others promises to be well worth the effort.

In many ways, this realization brings us full circle. One reason why meditation increases compassion is that it fosters equanimity. In the Buddhist sense, equanimity means not just composure or calmness but rather a mental state that reduces tensions by helping one realize the shared humanity and importance of all people. Meditation begins to slow and finally end the mind's tendency to separate people into different categories: white, black, rich, poor, friend, foe. The result is that everyone comes to be seen as equally valued and equally linked. And as we've just seen, creating a link with people is all that's needed to feel more compassion for them. In actuality, the tapping task — or any method you use to find similarity with another — is a shortcut: a way to game the system. It allows you to direct the mind to do what meditation would make automatic, leading to similar results.

Fortunately, the same rules apply even when the other in question is the future self. As we saw in the work of Bailenson and Hershfield in the beginning of this chapter, compassion for our future selves — wanting to make sure we're not penniless, ill, or otherwise unhappy — nudges us toward self-restraint. And unlike gratitude, we can actually feel compassion for our future selves; while they can't benefit us, we can certainly act to aid them. The obvious problem, though, is that as we've seen, most people don't often feel an affinity or link to their future selves. In essence, we all have an empathy gap with the future us. We accumulate debt rather than invest, party instead of work hard, or overeat instead of exercise, precisely because the costs seem so remote and will be borne by someone we can hardly imagine.

While virtual reality can help to bridge this gap in compassion, it's not a technology that most people have readily available. Practicing mindfulness can help, as any increase in compassion we feel, no matter whom we feel it for, boosts self-control. But the lack of compassion for a future self stems not only from feeling disassociated from that self — which meditation can also help counter — but from never getting the opportunity to see that person in distress. We need to make our future selves as real as we can and then try to take a walk in their shoes.

Yet in trying to imagine our future selves, it's important to avoid overly positive thinking. Just as the mind can engage in motivated reasoning to justify cheating, it can push us to imagine that everything's coming up roses for us decades down the line. The hope, of course, is that that will be the case. In order to work to ensure it, however, we need to look critically and prepare, much like Aesop's ant, for the possibility of hard times. We can recalibrate our sense of what is actually likely by taking an objective look at how those around us are managing old age, economically and otherwise, as well as from projections about retirement savings, the effects of unhealthy eating, and the like.

With that information in mind, it can be useful to take a half hour every so often to write a letter to, or at least have an imagined discussion with, our future selves. Many parents write letters to their children that are meant to be opened in years to come. And it's the compassion that they feel for them that motivates it: to explain choices, to give advice, express hopes and dreams for their success. But few people write letters to their future selves. Doing so, or even regularly imagining what we'd say, will force us to consider the well-being of our future selves — to *feel* for them — and thus to explain the choices that we're making in the present. It will help our minds cross the temporal barrier that separates us from our futures, thereby easing the way for compassion to flow and inspiring us to act in ways meant to preempt any distress we might be likely to experience in the years to come.

It's important to recognize, though, that temporal discussions can go both ways. While a future self can't talk to a present one, unlike the converse, a present self can belittle a past one. One additional strategy to consider, then, is to try to refrain from harshly admonishing or, even worse, shaming oneself for past failures, assuming they were well-intentioned tries. Feeling compassion for someone doesn't ever mean being a sucker. It doesn't mean excusing laziness, cheating, overeating, or any other seeming failure of self-control if there wasn't a true initial intent to succeed. What compassion does mean is forgiving failure when people, your own past self included, try to meet a goal but come up short. Recognizing whether a failure is an honest one or not, though, can be difficult. As we've seen, the conscious mind tends to cover up or rationalize its weaknesses when it comes to perseverance. One strategy, then, to try to clarify things is to search for any emotional tension — any pangs of guilt or regret that lie under the surface. Just as these were cues to people's whitewashed moral transgressions in my studies on cheating, so too can they indicate that other types of self-control failures stemmed from a less than honest effort.

To deal with this challenge I recommend two strategies. The first centers on getting clear-eyed about your own habitual style of self-talk. When you reflect on past failures, write down what you're thinking, or even better, verbalize and record your internal dialogue. This real-time record is much less vulnerable to subsequent interpretive biases. As such, it will offer important insight into whether and how you feel self-compassion. A second, related tactic is to set aside time once a week or so to reflect on a past failure where the effort to succeed was high, and then to forgive it. Choosing to condemn such failures — if that's what the first exercise reveals to be a typical response — will only foster shame and anxiety about future ones — two emotions that will themselves continually chip away at self-control. Using these strategies to uncover your own style and then, if needed, to cultivate self-compassion to change it will do just the opposite. Training our minds to make self-compassion the default response will not only increase self-control and grit going forward, it will also help make our bodies resilient in the face of stress.

Pride and Perseverance

Gratitude and compassion fit together well. Both are considered virtues. Both are universally seen as positive. They can even work hand in hand. One person helps another out of compassion for his plight, and then the second feels grateful and returns a favor in the future. Up to now, I've been arguing that socially oriented emotions — the ones that help us navigate the give and take of social living — can be coopted to help us achieve our own individual goals. By making our minds value the future, emotions such as gratitude and compassion make us more patient, more willing to persevere in the face of challenges, and more resistant to temptations that distract us from our aims. That is, compassion and gratitude build self-control. But pride somehow feels different. It feels self-centered, like it's all about *me*.

What seems to drive it is that *I* care that *I'm* good at something. After all, a person can be proud of just about any ability regardless of whether others find it admirable or useful. Some, for example, are proud of their abilities to read ancient Sanskrit, some of their abilities to cut through an aspen log with an ax in under twenty seconds, and some to imitate the call of a hog better than anyone else.

But pride's seeming self-focused nature isn't the only reason it might appear to be a strange choice to bolster self-control. While for some, such as top athletes, pride might require continued efforts to maintain one's skills and, thereby, one's status, for many others pride can simply signify that a goal has been reached. A person is good at something and recognized for it; there's no reason to work hard to be better. In fact, if you think about people who are labeled *proud,* likely many aren't viewed as diligent and dedicated. They're just as likely to be seen as egotists or blowhards. Pride, in the eyes of many, includes a bit of arrogance. And any state blemished by hubris and conceit isn't likely to be categorized as noble, a point bolstered by its absence on most lists of virtues. Quite the contrary, it tops the list of the seven deadly sins, which might explain the familiar proverb *"Pride comes before a fall."*

But this picture is too simplistic. Pride can lead to self-control and success; it *can* be a virtue. This isn't to say that those seemingly problematic beliefs about pride aren't true in some respects or in some situations, but rather that they stem from a unique quirk in pride that allows both its original purpose and useful elements to be obscured. In its most beneficial form, pride, like gratitude and compassion, is inherently social. And like them, it can help us achieve our goals. But before I begin offering proof of exactly how and why this is so, it's worth stepping back to explore pride's true nature.

FROM THE OUTSIDE LOOKING IN

One of the unique aspects of social living is that efforts can be divided. If one person in a group is good at hunting and another expert at cooking, then both will eat quite well. Social living allows and in fact encourages people to hone specific skills, even at the cost of not acquiring others, so that everyone in a close-knit group can benefit. But in a world of divided labor, it's not always immediately clear to people which sets of skills will be most valued. It's for this reason that pride evolved.

Historically, the skills that mattered were the ones that allowed a group to survive. This meant that the value of skills was determined by what a group needed at any given time. If war was imminent, abilities to fight or forge weapons would be an asset. In times of falling food production, being skilled at farming would be prized. As a result, the human mind is specially attuned to the views of others when it comes to determining self-worth. It's kind of like using crowdsourcing to determine value. As the eminent psychologist Leon Festinger described in developing social comparison theory, all people possess a fundamental drive to evaluate their abilities. We all want to know where we stand. While an easy way to do this in the modern world is to look for objective criteria (for example, test scores, performance evaluations), objective information isn't always readily available. The ability in question might be difficult to quantify, or historically speaking, scoring instruments might not have existed. In these cases, Festinger argued, people use the next best tool available: the opinions of others. If they want to know (a) what they should be good at, and (b) where they stand with respect to a valued ability, they look around. If they're receiving admiration from others for an ability, they know it's one that matters, not only in its own right but because it raises their status as a potential partner.

It's this latter piece — the one that ties abilities to a person's value as a partner — that results in the second facet of Festinger's social comparison theory: a drive for self-enhancement. Since cooperation with and social support from others play a role in success, it follows that any ability that increases a person's value is one for which it's worth accepting immediate short-term costs in time and effort to develop and show. Praise marks those abilities. An excellent hunter or craftsman receives praise for his skills. A person who could make a valuable tool, or discern information from the world around her in a unique way, would be heralded. And in reality, it's the resulting praise that pushes people to develop certain capabilities that, to them, might not have been of much interest otherwise.

This need was pride's origin. We can see it for almost as far back in time as we can look. Take one of our closest biological relatives, chimpanzees, as a case in point. Chimps, like humans, not only pay attention to the abilities of other chimps to solve problems, but they choose to cooperate more frequently with the ones who are successful. So it should come as no surprise that the origins of the emotional expression of pride — expanded posture, head tilted upward — can be seen in primates, where it is used to signal possession of a special status or ability. These facts show that our closest primate relatives, like us, pay close attention to the abilities of others and express cues linked to pride to mark their own triumphs in the face of challenges. Those cues signal that they have what everyone else needs.

But there's still a missing piece in the puzzle: how to explain the fact that people can and often do take pride in abilities that really only matter to them. For instance, a person can feel proud about the two pounds he worked weeks to lose, or having learned how to write code to solve a math problem in C++. Sources of pride can be so idiosyncratic because of an evolutionary quirk. Humans have come to possess a singular mental ability: true self-awareness. We're aware of *ourselves,* and that means we can be our own audience. This ability allows us metaphorically to survey ourselves from the standpoint of a third party. As a result, we can root ourselves on or be our own harshest critics. And we can assign our abilities value just as a third party could. Suppose a person is interested in paleontology. She'd probably be impressed by fossil hunters who spend weeks digging in the dirt to uncover remains of gastropods that lived millennia ago. And while her friends or family might not care too much about a shell fragment she dug up on her last vacation, her ability to uncover that small find might make her swell with pride. By virtue of self-awareness, she can bask in her own glory.

The recent development of self-awareness — recent in an evolutionary sense — is what allows pride to take the form we more commonly associate with this emotion: a pride based on internalized values. As with any emotion, how it's evoked doesn't really matter. Once it's felt, it will shape the decisions that follow. So pride has come to operate from and for the self. And that's potentially a good thing, as it enables us to target the benefits of pride toward our own goals, not just what others deem important. But it also has a downside: an audience of one is more likely to offer biased feedback. If all we do is pay attention to ourselves, the information we get about how superior or inferior our skills are can become miscalibrated. We can begin to assume we're great or terrible at everything, making us either arrogant or depressed. In such cases, pride (or lack thereof) can go off the rails, which is why, unlike many emotions, pride is thought to have two forms: an authentic and a hubristic one.

For now, let's focus primarily on the adaptive version, which we feel based on skills we truly possess that can be objectively confirmed. This version produces two intriguing results. The first is that we can be made to feel proud, and thus work hard to pursue any ability whatsoever if other people value it. Second, feeling and expressing pride in a task makes us appear as attractive partners or leaders as opposed to bossy know-it-alls or arrogant jerks.

FORWARD HO!

As with gratitude and compassion, the crux of my argument here is that pride can alter the mind's computations in ways that enhance self-control when we're faced with temptations. That is, pride should push us to persevere in the face of difficulty to acquire skills that will benefit us in the long run. In these cases, self-control equals a willingness to keep going, no matter how difficult or tedious that going might be. But making the case that pride plays a role in fostering such dedication can pose a few problems. Maybe musicians actually enjoy practicing long hours. Maybe students are intrinsically interested in the subjects they're studying. In other words, maybe people feel proud of their abilities but that pride has nothing at all to do with why they persevere. They practice, study, or work hard because they find the task rewarding; pride is just an afterthought. There's no easy way to tell when people report feeling proud about doing things they like.

To solve the problem — to show that pride can make people persevere at something whether or not they enjoy it — Lisa Williams, a professor at the University of New South Wales, and I needed to design a clever experiment. We quickly realized that we'd have to make people take pride in an ability they didn't know they had, and couldn't have any interest in pursuing. That meant, as usual, we had to employ some stagecraft. We had to convince people they were good at something that others valued and that they, therefore, could take pride in. Only then could we determine if pride would translate into greater diligence in honing that ability. And since we also needed to be sure people didn't enjoy the work, it needed to be a bit annoying.

To this end, we brought people into our lab under the pretext of studying their "visuospatial" ability. None of them had any sense of where they ranked in terms of visuospatial skills, or even what that really meant. And in truth, they didn't much care. Telling most people that their ability to recognize different shades of green was exceptional probably wouldn't be a major boost to their self-esteem. So improving this ability wasn't top on their list.

At the start of the experiment, then, we had a group of relatively uninterested, unmotivated participants who wanted nothing more than to get the whole thing over with as quickly as possible.

The experiment itself was simple. We told people we'd assess their visuospatial ability using a computerized task and then ask them to work on a second, related measure of visuospatial ability that would allow them to build their skills while measuring their improvement. The first task was relatively painless. Arrays of colored dots would appear briefly on the screen, after which people would have to report how many of the dots were red. This test was designed to be just difficult enough that people would believe it was doable but wouldn't have a great sense of how accurately they had performed. The reason for this feature will become clear in a minute.

The second visuospatial task was quite different. It involved mental rotation — something that most people find onerous. On each trial, two three-dimensional shapes would appear on the screen, and people had to make one of three choices: (1) the shape on the right was a rotated form of the shape on the left, (2) the shape on the right was not a rotated form of the shape on the left (that is, it was a different object), or (3) I quit. In reality, it was only the third one that we cared about. Since we had told people that they only had to work on this second task for as long as they wanted, what we were truly interested in was their level of perseverance. We wanted to know how long they would keep working to build and test their skills by choosing to complete additional problems rather than throw in the towel.

The analog of this setup is obvious. A person takes a test to gauge an ability and then has a chance to continue to grow and show that ability. It's a situation quite similar to most academic or professional training endeavors. But there was one thing missing: motivation to keep going. And that's where we expected pride to come in. The only remaining issue was how to get people to feel pride about their visuospatial ability. And to do that, we leveraged pride's social aspects. If people weren't going to be proud of their skills on their own — and let's face it, no one brags about their visuospatial abilities — we needed to convince them it was something worth caring about. The easiest way to do that was to let them know that other people were impressed by these skills.

To make this happen, we inserted one additional element into the experiment, between the first and second tasks. After each person finished the first visuospatial test — the one that involved counting red dots — she was brought into a different room to meet with the experimenter. In the neutral, or control, condition, she simply signed a form and then went back to work on the mental rotation task. In the pride condition, however, the subject was greeted by an experimenter who presented a score sheet indicating a visuospatial ability in the ninety-fourth percentile (that is, better than 94 percent of the general population). This was why we didn't want people to be able to guess exactly how well they had performed; we needed to give them false feedback that they would believe. In addition to giving this score information, the experimenter also smiled, looked impressed, and said something like "Wow! That was an amazing score" before patting the participant on the back and sending her back to complete the mental rotation task.

At this point we had two types of participants. Some were feeling quite proud — as confirmed by a subsequent report of their emotional states — and others were feeling as they usually do going about their days. What we wanted to know, of course, was whether those who were feeling proud would show greater perseverance in working on the next task. But there was one last possibility we needed to consider: Might people work longer not because they were feeling proud but because they simply thought they could succeed? Beginning in the 1970s, Stanford psychologist Albert Bandura demonstrated that believing they had the skills required to meet a challenge — something he termed *self-efficacy* — could, by itself, increase people's motivation to do so. And while the participants to whom we gave positive feedback were feeling proud, they also now held a belief that they possessed the skills needed to perform well. This information was part and parcel of inducing pride.

To rule out self-efficacy as a source of motivation, we needed to let people know how well they did in a way that didn't also make them feel very proud. Our focus on an ability that no one usually cared about made this easy. Whereas a third of our participants received no feedback, and a third received feedback meant to induce pride, the final third got feedback on their scores but without any praise. When they entered the experimenter's room one by one, she handed them the same score sheet she gave to the proud people (that is, indicating a score in the ninety-fourth percentile) but didn't give any verbal or nonverbal expressions of admiration. We reasoned that these people would know they did well but wouldn't feel very proud of their performance since neither they nor anyone else seemed to think the ability in question was an important one.

What happened next was exactly what we expected. People who were feeling proud of their abilities significantly increased their efforts while working on the difficult mental rotation task. They upped the time devoted to building their skills by 40 percent compared with people who weren't proud. Even more interesting was that self-efficacy didn't appear to play any role. Those who believed they possessed the ability to succeed — people who received the positive score feedback without any social acclaim — didn't persevere any longer than did those who received no feedback at all.

To be certain we had a handle on the psychological impact of pride, we ran the experiment a second time with another minor twist. Because we wanted to ensure that increased perseverance wasn't simply due to a good mood — as feeling pride is undeniably a positive experience — we replaced the self-efficacy condition with a happiness one. As you might expect based on our earlier work, happiness didn't much matter. While those feeling pride again showed an increase in perseverance, those feeling happy didn't devote any more effort to developing their skills than did those who were feeling nothing in particular. Pride was the only factor that increased effort. The more pride a person felt, the longer he resisted the temptation to give up.

When we look outside the confines of the lab, we can see how pride can manifest in the workplace. For example, feeling pride has been shown to increase effort and success in salespeople. Those who more regularly feel proud in their daily lives are more resilient in the face of initial challenges to moving products and, ultimately, better at sealing a deal. In a similar vein, the anticipation of future pride has been shown to increase dedication and performance in races for long-distance runners and in grade point averages for college students. But perhaps some of the best evidence comes from an experiment led by psychologist Wilhelm Hofmann, whose team tracked people in their daily lives using a technique known as experience sampling. This technique lets researchers collect data from people at specific points throughout the day. In Hofmann's study, participants were buzzed seven times a day by their smartphones and asked if they had recently experienced any temptations they tried to avoid: to procrastinate, overeat, drink alcohol, take drugs, sleep, et cetera. If they had recently experienced a temptation, they were also asked about their emotional states and whether their attempts at self-control had been effective. In line with the findings from my lab, Hofmann's results showed that pride increased self-control. The instances in which people reported feeling more pride directly corresponded to the ones in which they resisted tempting and pleasurable behaviors that might have otherwise distracted them from their goals. Not exactly what you'd expect from an emotion on the list of deadly sins.

Taken together, these findings suggest that pride, much like the other socially oriented emotions, nudges the mind to value the future. It makes people more patient, more motivated to accept costs and, thereby, reach valued goals. Recent findings by National University of Singapore psychologist Eddie Tong and colleagues confirms exactly this fact. Using an economic decision-making task similar to the one I used in my work on discounting, Tong's team showed that when pride is experienced in an appropriate context (that is, when not hubristic), it reduces the discounting of future rewards in a manner similar to gratitude. The result, as we can see in the findings on perseverance, is nothing short of enhanced self-control. Pride doesn't precede a fall; it fosters diligence and dedication.

Yet for all the links to self-control, I still haven't addressed the problem of likability. For my view to be correct, feeling and expressing pride has to make people more attractive as partners, not less. Increased self-control that makes others shun a person because of arrogance wouldn't do anyone much good.

I'll Take You

When it comes to picking a partner to work with, trust matters. Good partners are ones who can be relied upon. But the idea of trustworthiness itself rests on two intertwined factors. The first is integrity: Can I trust that someone will be fair and honest? The second is competence: Does the person actually have the abilities to do what's needed? One without the other is a recipe for trouble. A person might have every intention to help, but if he doesn't have the requisite skills, he won't help at all. While most people would trust their best friend to pick them up at the airport, they likely wouldn't rely on their best friend to remove a brain tumor unless she's a neurosurgeon. It's not that she wouldn't try like hell to safely remove the tumor; it's just that she wouldn't know where to start.

When people are searching for a partner, their chief criteria are competence and integrity. And as a result, the human mind is primed to seek evidence of these traits. In the case of integrity, we often use self-control as a proxy. Those who are viewed as being able to resist temptation and persevere in the face of difficulties are perceived as better bets to work with. And so when pride increases diligence, half the trustworthiness problem is solved; integrity is assumed.

This brings us to the issue of competence. University of British Columbia psychologist Jessica Tracy has long examined how proud people are perceived. Time and again her research shows that the nonverbal signals of pride — an expanded posture, a puffed-out chest, and an upward-tilted head — are read by others as signals of competence and status.

To put that idea to the test, Lisa Williams and I made an important tweak to our previous experiment that linked pride to perseverance. This time, rather than examine how pride affected efforts on a task done in isolation, we sat people down around a table in groups of three to work together. Each triad consisted of (a) someone who had just received acclaim in private for their visuospatial abilities, (b) someone who had received no feedback, and (c) an actor who worked for us. No one knew anything about the other two people in their group, but one of those people entered the situation feeling proud.

The experimenter, Lisa in this case, would then give the group their instructions for the next task. She presented a cube-shaped puzzle that she quickly twisted so as to make it a straight rod (the cube was made up of many smaller cubes that were all connected at different corners so it could be twisted into many different shapes). She placed the puzzle on the table and told the group that their goal was to work together to solve it by manipulating the pieces back together to re-form the larger cube in the ten minutes allotted. Trust me, this was no easy task. Lisa then left the room, at which point the actor always grabbed the puzzle, worked on it for a minute, and then put it back down.

Over the next nine minutes, a consistent pattern emerged. People feeling pride rose to prominence. Not only did they show greater dedication by working on the puzzle longer than did the participant in their group who wasn't feeling proud, they also gave that participant more advice and encouragement. This much we might have expected based on our earlier findings. But here we were really interested in how the expression of confidence and assertiveness was perceived.

As we anticipated, it put the proud people in a positive light. When we asked our participants who they thought was more of a leader in the groups, proud people received the highest ratings. When we asked them how much they liked the other people in their groups, the proud people always came out on top. This confirms not only that the proud people tried harder to solve the difficult puzzle, they did it in a way that stoked admiration and made others willing to work with them, to accept their advice, and, of most import, to want to do so again. Pride was a magnet, not a repellent. It was a signal, in both body language and behavior, that these people could be relied upon.

In reality, though, it's important to remember that the whole setup was an illusion. Those who entered the situation feeling proud were unknowingly doing so under false pretenses. We tricked them into believing they possessed a valued ability when they didn't, meaning that had we not capped the session at ten minutes, it's quite likely the picture would have dramatically changed. As time went on, it would have become clear that the proud people didn't actually possess any special expertise. Their efforts and advice wouldn't have been more likely to yield results than would have those of others. At that point, we might have witnessed the turn of pride toward that metaphorical fall. When it became obvious that a person's pride might be misplaced, it would turn to hubris and her appeal would crater. By design, though, our participants believed they possessed the necessary expertise, and as a result, the pride they exuded was authentic.

IN PRAISE OF PRIDE

As we've just seen, praise can engender pride, and pride can engender perseverance. What this means, of course, is that where we choose to direct our efforts is not entirely under our own control. We can be our own audience and self-direct our goals, but we also can take a cue from those around us. Given the social nature and adaptive purpose of pride, this makes good sense. Yet it's also true that most of us don't regularly alter our goals as we change our partners. We're not aiming to be a surgeon one minute and a top athlete the next even as we move among friends who might value one or the other set of abilities. So while it's true that the mind is sensitive to what others value, the process of internalizing those goals so that they chronically rise to the fore in different situations is usually complicated. To understand how this works, we need to take a brief detour to clarify the differences between two types of motivation: extrinsic and intrinsic.

Extrinsic motivation, as the name suggests, is a drive to garner an external reward. The legions of people who commute every day to work at jobs they despise know this type of motivation quite well. They work to get money, not because they enjoy the job itself. If the rewards suddenly disappeared or seemed unattainable, so too would the motivation that drove them to accept or endure the required steps along the way. On the flip side is intrinsic motivation. Here people act because they find the actions to be valuable and interesting in and of themselves. The student or employee who spends hours to solve an engineering problem because she's intrigued by it and finds the challenge exciting is intrinsically motivated. The one who does it in hopes of getting an A or a promotion is extrinsically motivated. In the absence of an academic or financial reward, the former will keep going while the latter would readily drop the task.

Although there's a lot of work out there examining the differences between these two types of motivation, much of it derives from a famous experiment conducted by Stanford psychologist Mark Lepper in the 1970s. Recognizing that parents believed rewards motivated children, Lepper decided to figure out whether dangling a prize in front of them actually proved effective in instilling long-term motivation. To do so, he divided a room of preschoolers, all of whom enjoyed drawing, into three groups. In the first — the expected reward condition — children were told they'd receive a special certificate with a gold seal on it if they were willing to draw a picture for the experimenter. In the second — the surprise reward condition — the kids ended up getting the same certificate, but they weren't told about it in advance. They just agreed to draw and were then surprised with the reward afterward. In the third — the no-reward condition — no reward was mentioned and no reward was received. The kids were simply invited to draw for the experimenter.

During the next several days, the researchers watched the children draw from behind one-way mirrors. The results were nothing short of surprising (at least at the time). The children in the no-reward condition drew about as much as did those in the surprise reward condition; both spent about 17 percent of their free time sketching at tables. But those in the expected reward condition behaved very differently. After receiving their special certificate, they drew much less, devoting only about 8 percent of their free time to it. This finding suggests that the kids came to reinterpret their interest in drawing as being driven by their interest in a reward. The kids in the surprise reward condition couldn't attribute their agreement to draw to anticipation of a reward because they didn't know about the certificate when they began. In that sense, their performance mirrored that of the children in the no-reward condition. But the ones who knew about the reward came to justify their subsequent efforts in light of it. On the days where the opportunity to receive an external award evaporated (that is, the days after they received the reward for drawing a picture), so too did their motivation. The upshot was rather depressing, as not only did rewards appear to diminish effort in the long run, they actually did so even for behaviors that had previously been intrinsically interesting.

In the decades since Lepper conducted his experiment, this negative view of tangible rewards has only grown, and with good reason. Hundreds of studies of material rewards in many realms (academic, athletic, professional, health) have shown this strategy to be ineffective. Even when material rewards are used to mark superior performance, they regularly diminish people's intrinsic motivation to succeed over time. We're all happy enough to chase the carrot, but once it's removed, so is any desire to achieve. Like the children in Lepper's study, we can come to view effort as focused on the external reward, even if that wasn't originally the case.

Praise works differently. It doesn't increase extrinsic motivation;

it creates an intrinsic one. While it's certainly true that praise can be experienced as a reward, it's just as true that it's not a *tangible* one. Unlike candy or gifts, praise of others can't be held in your hands. Its locus is internal. This one fact significantly alters how praise affects motivation. This isn't to say that praise can never be an enemy of long-term motivation. As with the pride (or hubris) it produces, the benefits of praise depend on how and when it's employed. The key to unlocking its power rests, like so much that has to do with self-control, on understanding how it links to our need for social connection.

Few psychologists are more renowned for illuminating human motivation than Edward Deci and Richard Ryan. Over decades of research, the duo has shown that robust motivation — the kind that springs from intrinsic interest and dedication — rests upon three pillars: competence, autonomy, and relatedness. We all enter this world with an innate motivation to explore it, understand it, and master it. Yet there's little doubt that maintaining and enhancing the motivation necessary to succeed requires specific conditions. And here, according to Deci and Ryan's work, is where these three pillars come into play.

For people to be intrinsically motivated to pursue a goal, they must first feel that they're getting more competent. They don't have to believe they're experts, but only that they are advancing in the skills that will ultimately be required to reach their goals. In other words, people can take pride in their initial successes, even if those successes are baby steps, and that pride, as we've seen, will drive them to continue to build their skills. But if improvement never materializes — if a person's ability to solve quadratic equations or play the piano never got better no matter the effort — it's likely that she will lose motivation to try. As we saw in the case of temporal discounting, favoring immediate satisfaction makes great sense if future rewards are unlikely.

The second requirement for intrinsic motivation is autonomy. Competence will only grow motivation if it's accompanied by a sense of being in control of decisions. If an adolescent studies or practices an instrument because his parents force him or promised him a reward, intrinsic motivation won't arise. As we've seen, these tactics don't aid in internalizing interest, meaning that if the teen can get away without expending effort to study or practice, he likely will. Abundant research shows that kids with teachers who encourage autonomy in learning, as opposed to ones who use controlling tactics to motivate their students, show greater intrinsic motivation in their academic work down the line. The same goes for parenting. Children whose parents are controlling in directing their activities end up showing less intrinsic motivation to achieve, irrespective of the domain (for example, sports, music). This is important, as less intrinsic motivation means less grit and self-control. Intrinsic motivation means the future is valued, and with that value comes a greater ability to avoid the distractions and temptations posed by procrastination and a focus on extraneous, immediate pleasures.

While these two pillars may seem somewhat obvious, the third — relatedness — is where I believe the action truly is and where pride really comes into play. Deci and Ryan argue, correctly in my opinion, that feelings of relatedness strongly bear on how other factors support motivation. As they point out, this phenomenon can already be seen quite early in life. John Bowlby's work on attachment styles demonstrated that toddlers who were more securely attached to their mothers — meaning they had a sense that they could rely on their mothers for support — were more ready and willing to engage in active exploration of their environs compared with those who were more anxious about their mothers' devotion. It's a pattern that plays out in all stages of life. For example, research has confirmed that students in classrooms led by teachers who are warm and caring regularly show higher levels of intrinsic motivation. Likewise, feelings of social inclusion, as we'll see in the next chapter, have been shown to foster greater perseverance and success among college students. Put simply, we work smarter, better, and longer when we're in the company of attentive others. And as we've seen, feeling and expressing pride draws others to us; it makes them want to work with us and, in so doing, reinforces our own efforts.

All this makes sense, but it still doesn't quite address the question of how people come to internalize the motivation to succeed via pride. That is, when and how pride, and the praise that leads to it, help people figure out what exactly to value, and thus pursue, in the first place. Initially, we all possess a desire to achieve. But as we've seen, what makes us proud of getting an A in school, an award at work, or a win on the court doesn't stem from biology. The brain doesn't come hardwired to care, or even know, about grades, sports, musical instruments, or the like. We're often proud because we look to our peers. As I noted in describing Festinger's social comparison theory and as shown in my experiments on pride, we look to others to figure out what's important, and it's praise that carries the message. Praise provides a key to understanding how and why certain motives can move from extrinsic to intrinsic — a process Deci and Ryan refer to as *internalization*. And while internalization clearly begins in childhood based on the reactions of our parents, it continues throughout life. We're constantly thinking about and responding to the praise we receive from spouses, bosses, teachers, and coaches. Some of it, depending on how much we identify with and value its source, can embed itself deeply into our consciousness, so much so that it ultimately becomes fused with our own sense of self. And in so doing, that praise births an intrinsic goal — one that we're now willing to pursue because it has become important to *us*.

In my experiments on pride we were able to increase people's motivations to work on their visuospatial abilities, but in truth, that effect likely dissipated once they left the lab. The finding was important because it proved that pride could lead to a direct increase in perseverance. Making that motivation stick, however, would have required a much stronger personal relationship. Those participants would have to have truly cared about the experimenter's views in a way similar to that of other important people in their lives. Only then would it lead to true internalization of a goal.

If this process sounds somewhat familiar, it should. One type of internalization can go by a more common name: peer pressure. The human desire to fit in is so strong that we often come to embody the traits and motives that important people around us value. And although most people flinch at the mention of peer pressure, in reality it is neither inherently good nor bad; it all depends on the peers. If one's peers are fashionistas who value consumerism, or "losers," for lack of a better term, who embrace an ethos of sloth or overindulgence, sure, peer pressure can be detrimental to self-control. On the other hand, many people learn some of their best virtues through peer pressure. We learn to be noble because we're praised and valued for it by those we care about. We learn patience and honor because we're shunned or looked down upon by others we admire when we fail to demonstrate these traits. Virtuous societies transmit good character *through* peer pressure, not in spite of it. The idea that individualism — the rejection of any influence of group norms — is always good just isn't correct; a knee-jerk reaction against socialization by the group misses the point. Praise, because it's a currency of social value unlike material rewards, is a prime force in motivating us to internalize goals, which, when the goals are virtuous, can make us accept many immediate costs for future gain.

To see the strength of such peer pressure, let's look at the case of a group of people who struggle mightily with intertemporal trade-offs on a daily basis: addicts. Whether they're hooked on drugs, food, sex, or shopping, addicts are united by a common dilemma: they routinely engage in behaviors that bring short-term pleasure and long-term ruin. And while there are many therapies designed to help (it's interesting to note that almost none of them rely on will-power, which again suggests its limitations), perhaps the most fundamental and widely used is quite social in nature: group support. The backing and praise an addict receives from others in the group for remaining clean provide a powerful impetus to resist temptation. In reality, this positive group support is nothing less than peer pressure. So while it's certainly true that peer pressure can offer a route into substance abuse, so, too, can it boost self-control to help offer a way out.

Avoiding the Slippery Slope

Using pride wisely requires a solid grasp of when and why it can go wrong. While any emotion can be problematic if experienced in the wrong intensity or in an inappropriate context, pride is potentially more problematic than other emotions because it's the most susceptible to these errors, particularly the halo effect.

As its name implies, the halo effect causes people to see virtue where it might not be justified. When medieval and Renaissance painters placed a glowing, golden circle above a subject's head, observers took it to signify that this person was special; she was saintly and, therefore, so too were *all* of her qualities. In the human mind, the halo effect works in a similar way. It's a type of confirmation bias in which once we come to believe a person possesses superior characteristics in one domain, we generalize that belief, often erroneously, to others. Put another way, because we believe a good person has good qualities, we come to interpret all that person's actions or traits in a positive light. For example, supervisors assume an employee who shows enthusiasm is also competent. Likewise, most adults expect that someone who is attractive will also be intelligent. This cognitive bias matters for pride because, as I noted earlier, humans possess the relatively rare ability to be their own audience. As a consequence, we're just as likely to succumb to the halo effect when evaluating our own qualities as when evaluating those of others. This is where the slippery slope to hubris begins.

Whereas authentic pride — pride that stems from proven possession of a valued ability — is often narrowly defined, hubristic pride is just the opposite. It's a grandiose belief that one has prized qualities that one doesn't actually have. The result is that the benefits of pride become quite short-lived. As those around a hubristic person begin to see that his pride isn't warranted, views of his character fade fast.

Pride, unlike hubris, can have positive qualities that earn it the right to be grouped with compassion and gratitude. For example, a doctor can take pride in learning new diagnostic or surgical skills as she will now also be able to use them in a helpful way. There is no tension here between pride and the other socially focused emotions. However, if people aren't cognizant of all the hard work and support necessary to achieve a goal — if they believe an ability derives solely from their intrinsic greatness — it will ultimately diminish the desire to practice and progress.

It shouldn't be a surprise that these differing types of pride produce different outcomes. In studying a thousand people, a team led by University of Miami psychologist Charles Carver found that those who habitually experience authentic pride have greater self-control, perseverance, and goal attainment. Those who frequently experience hubris, though, tend to be more impulsive and motivated solely by monetary or related external rewards.

The differences between authentic and hubristic pride don't end with motivation, however. Hubristic pride also tends to be associated with a fragile ego, and by anxiety and aggressive tendencies as people strive to keep up the illusion of competence and control. Authentic pride, on the other hand, is associated with increased social support, lower anxiety, and a greater desire to help others by sharing one's expertise. We can see similar patterns even at the neurobiological level. Whereas hubristic behaviors are often accompanied by elevated testosterone, those related to authentic pride (for example, mentoring and outreach) are accompanied by lower testosterone and, more important, higher serotonin, which is associated with increased motives for bonding and social support, as well as feelings of well-being.

For pride to work, it must be paired with humility — a humility to know that no matter our skill set, each of us depends on what others have to offer. When we're admired for our expertise, it's usually because we're willing to share it, not because we lord it over those around us. And since none of us can be an expert in all areas, we must be humble enough to recognize that we *cannot* be great at everything; there will be times when we need to rely on others. People who follow this advice are the ones for whom pride, like gratitude and compassion, becomes virtue, not vice.

The ability to see ourselves from a third-person vantage point gives us another opportunity to use pride effectively. We can be not only our own audience but our own prognosticator. That is, we can be alert to the pride we're feeling and look forward to the pride we're yet to feel. As it turns out, anticipatory pride can be just as effective a motivator as its real-time counterpart. Research by Vanessa Patrick of the University of Houston's Bauer College of Business proves the point. Patrick conducted an experiment in which she placed a piece of cake in front of people who were trying to lose weight. She told one-third of them to think about the pride they might feel in not eating all the cake, another third to think about the shame they might feel if they ate all the cake, and, importantly, the final third to think about nothing in particular (that is, she didn't say anything to them about the cake). She then left them alone to eat what they liked and, after they had left, weighed the pieces of cake to get a precise measure of exactly what each person had consumed.

Anticipating pride proved quite beneficial for bolstering self-control. A full 40 percent of those focused on feeling future pride resisted taking even a single bite of cake, whereas only 19 percent of those in the control condition (that is, those not told to anticipate any emotion) and 11 percent of those in the shame condition did the same. Even if we look at those who did eat some cake, the benefits of pride are apparent. Where those anticipating pride consumed only 1.2 ounces of cake on average, those in the control and shame conditions ate more than double that amount.

One strategy for using pride in our own lives is to keep a journal where we track our success and our aspirations. Just as we should feel compassion for ourselves if and when we miss a goal, we should take pride when we successfully take steps toward a goal, as well as anticipate the pride we'll feel when reaching the next step. By doing this, we'll be charting our advancement through time, with today's achievement likely being yesterday's aspiration. At each step, then, it can be quite motivating to feel the relevant pride, much more so than if we only allowed ourselves to be proud upon reaching a final goal. However, it's also essential to remember that progress toward goals doesn't always follow a linear trajectory. It often goes in fits and starts. What matters most is a continued upward trajectory irrespective of the rate. Taking pride in the direction of progress benefits perseverance most.

Still, to be effective, we must offer praise in exactly the right ways. First, it has to be perceived as sincere. If people are praised for doing something easy — something for which they could be expected to succeed — the acclaim, as well as the person offering it, loses credibility. Whether we're talking to ourselves or to a child or peer, we shouldn't use praise as a throwaway. Saying "good job" mindlessly not only renders it meaningless, it actually makes it harder for us to be taken seriously when our praise is heartfelt. In a similar vein, praise should be reserved for goals or behaviors that actually require some specialized ability or effort. That doesn't mean it need be reserved until someone reaches the pinnacle of said ability, but rather it might be held until noticeable effort and progress have been made. If we offer praise for any old thing — from putting away the laundry to mowing the lawn — we impede its ability to guide us toward goals that truly matter. Why work hard to achieve something if similar praise and a sense of status and belonging can come from doing something much more mundane?

Second, praise should focus on effort, not ability. Effort-based praise (for example, I'm proud of you because you're working hard), as opposed to ability-based praise (for example, I'm proud of you because you're smart) ends up being more robust. When failure comes, ability-based praise can reduce intrinsic motivation because people suddenly feel like they might not have the valued ability they thought they had after all. However, with effort-based praise they can simply try again, as it is still entirely possible that their future efforts will pay off. Here again, it's a situation akin to Dweck's idea of a growth mindset. Praise for effort reinforces the belief that efforts — not immediate success in an endeavor — are worthwhile, while praise for a specific ability reinforces the notion that if that ability suddenly evaporates, all might be lost.

Finally, praise needs to foster a sense of autonomy. It needs to be central to the goal, not external to it. For example, praising someone for showing initiative in working toward a valued end is beneficial. Praising someone for working to gain a reward (for example, a parent saying, "I'm impressed you're working hard to get that new video game I promised to buy you if you got your grades up") is not. For most of us, this means avoiding the tendency to resist offering praise for getting a carrot. Yes, getting a raise at work is a good thing, but feeling proud about solely the increased dollars won't go a long way to making you care more about your performance. I recognize that not everyone enjoys their work. And that constitutes a different problem. But for those who want to step up their own or others' achievement on their professional path, identifying an aspect of the job in which they can take pride (for example, how being a caring 911 operator helps callers in crisis) can make a substantial difference when it comes to motivation and satisfaction.

Part 3

VALUE ADDED

Being Social Means Being Successful

Throughout this book I've offered two interrelated arguments. The first is that behaving virtuously — being honest, fair, diligent, cooperative — leads to better outcomes down the line than does being immediately self-serving. The second is that morally toned emotions such as gratitude, compassion, and pride give us the self-control that builds relationships with others and benefits our own future selves. What I haven't yet said is that enhancing social relationships offers two additional boons. The first is that social bonds, on their own, build grit. The second is that they simultaneously help us combat one of the most painful plagues of modern life: loneliness.

Compassion, gratitude, and pride evolved to increase self-control because self-control undergirds virtuous behavior. Virtuous behavior, in turn, is worth enacting because it is essential to building social relationships that have historically led to success and happiness. Put simply, socially oriented emotions build self-control because having strong social relationships was self-control's original purpose. And so now, in cultivating these states, we can increase our motivations to act in ways that benefit others, including, perhaps most important, our own future selves, while at the same time helping to make us feel supported in the moment. To see how and why these arguments are valid requires a clear understanding of the dynamics involved. So before we consider the additional ways in which social relationships benefit success, it's worthwhile to show exactly why virtuous, as opposed to selfish, behavior truly is superior in a scientific sense.

MORALITY PAYS DIVIDENDS

The question of whether honesty and generosity pay is an old one. While philosophers and theologians have long argued in favor of this notion, there's no question that purely self-interested and Machiavellian tactics can at times appear useful as well. So when considering whether it's better to be a trustworthy cooperator or a deceptive cheater, we need to peer through a scientific lens.

At base, cooperation is an intertemporal dilemma. Like the marshmallow test, it presents options that hold different consequences as time passes. A person can choose to accept small costs now, perhaps from splitting profits with a partner, in order to get potentially larger gains later that might emerge from a thriving, long-term partnership. But there's a catch. Note that the word *potentially* lurks in the previous sentence, and with it, the notion of uncertainty — or a gamble — rears its head. The benefits of cooperation only accrue if the future gains actually happen, which here means if people are honest. If some people loaf, cheat, or otherwise don't hold up their end of the deal, being cooperative becomes precarious or worse.

An easy way to see the risks and benefits associated with cooperation comes from a slight alteration of a famous game known as the prisoner's dilemma. In the usual version, two criminals must make choices during individual interrogations about whether to keep quiet or sell their partner out. It's a game focused on how much there is to lose depending on whether people act to keep a promise or selfishly break it. The same rules apply, however, if we reframe the game in terms of wins. For example, if two people combine their resources by working together to make a product (that is, if they cooperate), let's say they can each earn $300 when they sell it. If on the other hand the two partners choose to compete, they'll earn $100 apiece instead, since they'll now need more individual resources. But if one unfairly competes — if he promises to work with his partner but then strikes out on his own after using joint resources — he can earn $500 and leave the other with nothing.

Deciding the best course of action can get a little complicated. At first blush, it might seem like the last choice makes the most sense — you'd end up with $500 versus $300. But there's a wrinkle here. It's not just one person making the decision; both partners are contemplating the same options. If they both go with what initially seems the most profitable strategy — if they both choose to compete — something strange happens. They end up worse off than if they both choose to cooperate: $100 each versus $300 each. And there's the rub. The only way to ensure joint success and satisfaction is to accept a smaller, shared gain. If they each choose to work in what appears to be their immediate self-interest, they eventually end up with less.

There is, of course, one other possibility that I haven't mentioned here. If one person could somehow predict that the other was going to cooperate, then competing on his part would seem to make the most sense. So if an unscrupulous person knew that a new partner had a sterling reputation, he should cheat him. There's no disputing this fact. In a single round of this game — a game whose structure was designed to match many dilemmas real life throws at us — giving in to a desire for an immediate gain, even at cost to another, is the way to win. There's a downside to this strategy, though: the person who cheats will quickly develop a reputation as someone not to be trusted, thereby limiting his opportunities for future gains.

Given this dynamic, it might seem that the question of whether competition or cooperation is better remains unanswered. Solving the conundrum requires adding one additional element to the equation: time. After all, using self-control to forestall bigger gains and cooperate only makes sense if the smaller gains of cooperation trump the bigger gains of competition over the long run.

It might seem that figuring out which strategy would win would necessitate following different people for decades. Not an easy, or even feasible, challenge, but luckily one the political scientist Robert Axelrod found a clever way around. While he couldn't tell people what strategy to choose and chart their fortunes over years, he could do the next best thing. Using computer simulations, he created "people" and made them play rounds of the prisoner's dilemma day and night using different strategies: forgive past transgressions, be vengeful, or be trustworthy every time, to name a few. He then charted each "person's" success over hundreds of interactions.

At the end of the day, the winner — the strategy that resulted in the greatest accumulation of points — was a deceptively simple one: tit for tat. As the name suggests, tit for tat (TFT) implies copying a partner's behavior. Although it starts out being cooperative, it quickly adjusts its decisions based on another's reputation. For instance, if a potential partner treated another fairly, the second partner would return the favor during the next interaction with the former; it would cooperate. If the first partner acted selfishly, it would follow suit and cheat the next time they met. While it's true that TFT didn't emerge victorious in every round, it was the strategy that fared the best on average. Although players acting more selfishly jumped ahead initially, their gains waned over time as others began to shun them. In contrast, players who chose to cooperate when it was wise to do so accumulated the most resources over many, many runs of the simulation, and ultimately, that's what drives evolutionary adaptation: a robust solution.

The primary reason TFT won is because those using it recognized the risks and benefits of cooperation. They were willing to accept smaller rewards in the moment for larger, longer-term gains when they seemed likely. In other words, TFTs were patient but not gullible.

Yet everything I've just said about the benefits of cooperation, while true, has the potential to raise something of a paradox. If cooperation is important to success — so important that we enter this world predisposed to build social relationships whenever possible — it might seem odd that cheating, lying, and loafing persist, given that they appear to offer less-than-optimal outcomes. The reason they remain is that a society of complete saints (or complete sinners, for that matter) wouldn't be evolutionarily stable. There would be way too much for any single person to gain by adopting the strategy that almost no one else was following. If, for example, a cheater entered a world where everyone else shared without hesitation, he'd clean up. So while simulations show that people who act selfishly can leap ahead in the early stages of interactions, they end up with fewer total gains at the ends of their lives as compared with slow and steady cooperators. After a while, the reputations of the selfish precede them, meaning that no one wants to be friends with them, work with them, or support them in any way, and as a result, their ability to flourish ebbs. Nonetheless, our minds are always on the lookout for those situations in which selfishness and cheating might give us a leg up. My experiments on cheating are a case in point.

When people believed they could get away with self-serving behavior, the need for self-control to adhere to the goals or standards they set for themselves became clear. Without it, they rationalized a way to embrace an immediate pleasure that went against their own professed standards.

For these reasons, morality is, as I noted, self-control's true *raison d'être*. When gratitude, compassion, or pride makes us behave nobly, it does so to ensure that we'll attract others to us — others who will support and work with us to achieve success. What's more, by making us value the future, these states also make us willing to work to benefit our own future selves. But in helping us to foster social relationships, these emotions also build grit in another, indirect way. We now turn toward that way.

Social Grit

Stanford psychologists Gregory Walton and Geoffrey Cohen might have found something of a magic bullet for educational success — a single ingredient that can increase students' perseverance by almost 50 percent. Walton and Cohen have long been interested in what drives academic achievement. Sure, factors such as intelligence and early education make a difference, but Walton and Cohen are among the growing cadre of education researchers who recognize that the human mind evolved to learn in a social environment, not in isolation. For millennia prior to industrialized schooling, we learned in interactive pairs or groups, stumbling and triumphing together. And as a result, our brain's mechanisms for perseverance are tuned for just such environs.

Walton and Cohen had a hunch that feelings of social connection on their own might play an important role in student motivation. To find out just how much, they conducted an experiment in which they asked students to work on mathematics puzzles. Unbeknownst to the poor students, the puzzles were unsolvable by design. The researchers weren't interested in how smart their subjects were; they wanted to discover how long the students would work on the problems placed before them. The researchers told their subjects they could devote as much or as little time to the puzzles as they liked, but beforehand, they asked them to read an article from *The Chronicle of Higher Education* that was supposedly written by a graduate of their university's math program who'd landed an enviable job after graduation.

There were actually two versions of the article, which described the joys of majoring in math. One focused on individual skills and achievements, the thrills of eureka moments and the satisfaction of scoring well on competitive exams. In the other version he emphasized the company of friends who studied theorems together and the encouragement and open-door policies of his math professors. The purpose of this chicanery was to frame the ongoing rewards of pursuing excellence in math as involving either individual skills or interpersonal relationships. While the ultimate reward was the same in each case — an interesting and well-paid job — the learning environment and rewards along the way were cast in very different lights.

After the students read one framing or the other, Walton and Cohen noted how long each persisted in the effort to solve the puzzles. After the researchers controlled for each student's math ability and general interest in mathematics (a student who hated math was probably was going to spend less time on math puzzles no matter what), it became very clear that the students who had read the social version of the article persevered longer on the problems than did those who had read the skill-based version. Framing the rewards in social terms increased the time people spent trying to solve the problems by almost 50 percent.

To really drive home the power of social connection in increasing perseverance, Walton and Cohen repeated the experiment, with a few twists. This time there was no article to read. Instead, the team manipulated the social nature of the math challenge by making some students believe they were part of an actual social group. Before the students set to work, some were told that they had been randomly assigned to be a member of a puzzles "group," while others were told that they were a puzzles "person" (that is, their score would be calculated individually). Those who received the *group* label were given the names of other people in their group (none of whom they had ever met) who would also be trying to solve math problems; those who got the *person* label received no such information. Now, the important point here was that all students — those in the team and in the individual conditions — would actually be working in a room alone. But those given the *group* label believed others would evaluate and were depending upon their work as part of a group effort.

Once again Walton and Cohen recorded how much time the students spent on that same set of unsolvable math puzzles, and once again the value of social connection shone through. The sense of being part of a team — even a team made up of strangers — led the students to persevere considerably longer. Not only that, but even after a week had passed, the students who thought they were part of a group continued to show increased motivation. When given the opportunity to work on challenging math puzzles by themselves or to engage in other, more enjoyable activities — a classic self-control dilemma — they chose the former much more often than did those who possessed no sense of group affiliation. Knowing they were part of something — having a goal that they knew was shared by a group and to which they could contribute and be valued — pushed people to work hard and resist immediate pleasures. In short, it gave them grit, and effortlessly so.

Perhaps most important, Walton and Cohen's lab-based findings translate well into the real world. Consider the gender disparity in STEM (science, technology, engineering, and mathematics) fields. The number of women completing bachelor's degrees in STEM fields is half that of men even though women make up about 56 percent of the U.S. college population. While this gender difference may have many causes, University of Massachusetts psychologists Tara Dennehy and Nilanjana Dasgupta wondered whether one of the factors that might discourage women was a reduced sense of belonging. It's well known that many women studying and working in STEM fields regularly report that these traditionally male-dominated domains can feel unfriendly or alien at times. To test their idea, Dennehy and Dasgupta enlisted 150 working engineers (both male and female) to serve as mentors to 150 female engineering students during their first year in college. As the researchers expected, the students who had women mentors were less likely to have dropped out of their engineering major (even a year after the mentoring had ended) than were those who had male mentors or no mentors at all. What's more, one of the biggest predictors for the students' ultimate success in their studies was a feeling of increased belonging that came from working with their mentor. Here again, a sense of affiliation and welcoming support boosted motivation and perseverance in the face of challenging work.

RESILIENT SUCCESS FOR BODY AND MIND

If feelings of attachment to others enhance self-control and perseverance, they should also reduce some of the stress associated with resisting temptation. As we saw earlier, the stress from continually, willfully trying to show grit can harm the body and mind.

To test this idea, Walton and Cohen wanted to see if a relatively simple intervention designed to increase feelings of social inclusion could also enhance the performance of those students who typically face the greatest costs to health when relying on willpower and similar cognitive techniques to strive for success: those from underprivileged backgrounds. Their plan was to follow two cohorts of new college students, one African American and one European American, through their pursuit of a bachelor's degree. They knew that many in the African American cohort entered prestigious colleges feeling a bit alienated from the majority of students and often attributed the regular feelings of loneliness and social adversity that come with entering college to themselves — to their being somehow different from most other students on their campus. Walton and Cohen believed that if they could alter these perceptions, they might be able to remedy some of the stresses typically associated with trying to succeed academically. That is, if they could help these students to realize their links and shared experiences with other students — the fact that everyone feels homesick and lonely early on — it could reduce their anxiety by encouraging them to form more friendships, which, as we've just seen, should enhance their academic performance.

During the second semester of their freshman year, the researchers brought half of the students in the study to their labs and gave them reading materials that discussed the sense of adversity, isolation, and social anxiety many freshmen feel. The materials also contained testimonials of students from the same university who described how these feelings began to fade over time as their social circles grew. To highlight their similarities with the purported authors of the essays, Walton and Cohen also asked the new students to write their own personal essays on how their experiences in college to date mirrored those described by the older students they had just read about. And finally, to drive the point home, the new students were asked to record a video where they'd read the essay they just wrote so that it could be shown as encouragement to other new students. For a week following this intervention (or, for the other half of students, who didn't receive the intervention, a week during the same period), everyone in the study completed daily surveys that measured their experiences and feelings of adversity to see if the interventions had taken hold.

Three years later Walton and Cohen reviewed the academic records of the students in the study and asked them to report on their long-term sense of social belonging, academic success, and well-being. The findings were impressive. The academic performance of those who had received the social-belonging intervention showed a steady increase year after year, to the degree that it tripled the percentage of African American students who earned GPAs in the top 25 percent of their class. And it was these same students — the ones with the greatest increase in academic success year to year — who early on showed greater feelings of belonging following the brief intervention during their freshman year. This finding suggests that when socially isolated people feel more similar to and connected with others, their ability to focus and persevere goes up, which in turn improves their resilience and achievement. Note that the intervention didn't produce similar effects for European American students. Because they didn't enter college feeling the same degree of isolation, their situations had little room for improvement.

But this isn't the end of the story. Those greater feelings of social inclusion and reduced stress brought better health too. African Americans who received the intervention reported feeling significantly better on average and visiting doctors less often compared with those in the control group. Here again, the link between social relationships, self-control, and mind-body health is clear. Social connection reduced stress and increased well-being among these students. My hunch is that the emotions people were feeling — which unfortunately remained unmeasured in the study — were also likely to have played an important role. We know from research reviewed earlier in this book that gratitude and compassion — which form the glue of social relationships — buffer the negative effects of stress. And as the social connections they support also soothe stress, the result is a mutually reinforcing one. When we spend time with close others, we experience gratitude, compassion, and related social emotions that bind us ever more strongly to one another, which also boosts health and well-being.

Clearly, gratitude, pride, and compassion enhance our social lives, and in so doing, they increase our motives for success through a secondary route as well. But in benefiting our social connections, they also help relieve what, for many, is one of the greatest threats to happiness in modern life: loneliness.

COMBATING THE RAVAGES OF LONELINESS

One of the dangers of using strictly cognitive tools for self-control is that we can too easily adopt a nose-to-the-grindstone focus on individual advancement. By ignoring self-control's links to social relationships, we can easily set up a robotic ideal for ourselves: the lone, ascetic workaholic. While some of the celebrated exemplars of grit can seem to have it all, others, the unsung but no less diligent, toil in isolation, cut off from the warm embrace of family and friends — an embrace that, as we'll see, is one of the things that matter most for happiness.

It may sound like I'm being a pessimist, or overblowing the risks of single-minded focus, but I don't think that's the case. After all, we've just seen how feeling connected to others can boost success, and we saw earlier how a gritty pursuit of practice can lead to the spinning of wheels in social isolation. Yet unfortunately, modern life is lonely for many. For all the pleasures relationships bring us, we're failing miserably at maintaining them. As Harvard political scientist Robert Putnam noted in his classic book *Bowling Alone,* the past few decades have witnessed significant drops in socializing. Attendance at club meetings has declined 58 percent, the time families spend eating dinner together has dropped 43 percent, and even the number of times people invite friends over is down 35 percent. Surveys by others tell a similar story. From 1985 to 2004, the number of people who felt that they had no one in their lives they trusted and with whom they could discuss important concerns nearly tripled. And while 80 percent of adults in 1985 reported they had at least one close friend, that figure dropped to 57 percent over the next twenty years. The result is that more than 53 percent of Americans regularly feel lonely, especially when working or away at school — the exact places where they're trying to achieve their professional goals.

While it's pretty clear that loneliness isn't pleasant, most of us fail to recognize how painful and debilitating it can be. In evolutionary terms, social isolation could be deadly, since humans relied so much on the group for their survival; hence the power of gratitude, pride, and compassion to build and maintain those bonds. And though today's human living alone might not die as quickly as her ancestor likely would have, the pain and damage that loneliness causes are real.

When I say loneliness is painful, I mean that in physical terms as well as emotional ones. In 2003 a team led by UCLA psychologist Naomi Eisenberger wanted to find out what a lonely brain looked like. The challenge was how to make someone feel lonely when inside an MRI scanner. The team adapted a typical playground slight to the virtual world. The game, known as cyberball, involves three "people" who appear on a computer screen: the true participant and two fake others (whom the true participant believes to be real). The rules of play are simple: when the virtual ball gets thrown to someone, that person has to pass it to one of the two other players. Social exclusion happens when two other players on the screen begin to throw the ball only to each other. This may sound like no big deal, but in experiment after experiment it has been shown to make those who are excluded feel alone and devalued. And because it requires only a computer monitor and two buttons to play the game, people can do it while inside a scanner.

The results of the experiment couldn't have been clearer. Those who were excluded in the game showed increased activity in brain areas known to respond to physical pain, meaning that loneliness feels physically painful. It actually hurts. Yet pain isn't its worst effect. Loneliness ravages the mind and body over time in ways science is only now beginning to understand.

Nobody has done more to illuminate this regrettable fact than University of Chicago psychologist John Cacioppo. For decades he has been studying the detrimental effects of isolation, and what he's uncovered has begun to raise alarms. When combined with findings such as those above showing the growing prevalence of loneliness, we can see the distinct possibility of a looming public health crisis. Persistent loneliness produces double the mortality risk of obesity. It's equivalent to smoking in terms of increasing the odds of an early death. It impairs immunity and increases inflammation, both of which are linked to maladies such as heart disease and diabetes. Over time, the chronic stress that accompanies loneliness also disrupts sleep, elevates blood pressure, and causes depression.

The link between loneliness and depression is so strong that feelings of isolation can cloud people's mood even when their social lives improve. For example, those who have been lonely for a year but then regain social connections still show deleterious effects. The experience of that earlier loneliness continues to darken their mood and worldview for months. Put simply, loneliness shapes our future. It can even do so by spreading within social networks. Feeling isolated in the moment has been shown to increase people's expectations that loneliness will continue. These expectations, in turn, tend to distort their views of others' willingness to accept them, making them turn ever more inward. And as they turn inward, others with whom they might normally interact begin to feel lonely too.

One of the clearest examples of this sad phenomenon can be seen in the famous Framingham Heart Study, which tracked thousands of people over decades. When the researchers looked to see where loneliness occurred, they found it in clusters — clusters that tended to grow over time almost as if the feeling were contagious. For example, if a person reported feeling isolated at time 1, some others in that person's social network — others who originally weren't feeling isolated at all — suddenly became lonely by time 2. And this "transmission" of loneliness could be directly traced from person to person within expanding social circles.

To the extent that any of us begins to devote greater effort to single-mindedly pursuing goals in ways that separate us from others, we're weakening our social bonds and opening ourselves to all the potentially deadly health and psychological effects associated with isolation. After all, isolation doesn't have to result from geographical separation. It can stem from time famine as well. Sitting next to your partner on the couch while you work on your laptop isn't social connection. In truth, it can be even worse than working in different locales, as the excuse that physical distance provides for being emotionally unavailable falls away.

Still, it is true that self-control has itself been linked to social success; the children who performed the best on Mischel's marshmallow test had better interpersonal relationships later in life. This might lead us to assume that an ability to delay gratification might itself afford protection from future isolation. In fact, it does so, up to a point. A capacity for self-control *can* help people build stronger relationships; to the extent that it makes one willing and able to share, to be honest, and the like, it can burnish your character. But *can* doesn't always mean *will*; it all depends on how that self-control is ultimately grown and used. If it's used in equal measures to foster achievement and social relationships, it will certainly reduce loneliness. But if it's wielded more asymmetrically — focused primarily on a person's own advancement — it can compound the problem.

This can even be true when the goal is a prosocial one, such as curing a disease or starting a charity. Devoting yourself to such a good cause at the expense of fostering your own individual social connections won't make you feel any closer to others than would designing a new type of computer display or managing a hedge fund. Sure, at the end of the day, one type of goal might benefit humanity more than another, but pursuing either can leave people eating dinner alone at their desk.

Unfortunately, but not surprisingly, the data bear this view out. As people rely more and more on executive function, willpower, and rationality to keep them focused on their individual goals and achievements, they spend less time connecting with others. In reviewing survey data from more than 100,000 Americans, psychologists Emily Bianchi and Kathleen Vohs found that as people climbed the ladder of success — here defined by household income — they spent less time socializing with friends and family.

Some might argue that this diminution of connection is the inevitable and understandable price of success. If people commit to pursuing a difficult goal, they might well have to structure their entire lives around that goal. They might have to block out and resist temptations or distractions by focusing their attention on the task at hand, and if that means spending more time alone in the short run, so be it. But what most people don't realize — especially the ones who might be readiest to proffer this argument — is that reducing social connection to pursue a goal often brings diminishing returns. As we've seen, loneliness itself directly limits the ability to control one's impulses, trapping people in a pernicious cycle of failure. As loneliness continues, the motivation and ability to exert cognitive control and use willpower-based strategies become more difficult to maintain. The upshot is that, over time, following this route actually increases the risk of failure in domains ranging from one's career (for example, completing projects or studying for a test) to health (keeping to a diet, avoiding alcohol). Two examples that show the diverse disadvantages of loneliness: it has been tied to lower scores on standardized tests and to reductions in exercise.

With respect to the professional realm, research by Hakan Ozcelik and Sigal Barsade that surveyed more than eight hundred employees and supervisors at two large organizations documents the negative outcomes associated with loneliness. At the start of the study, the team assessed loneliness through people's self-reports and those of their colleagues, who shared observations of their coworkers' degree of isolation. Six weeks later, the researchers collected information about the same employees' attitudes and performance levels from both their supervisors and themselves. As might now be expected, a clear link between loneliness and performance emerged. Those who were lonely showed not only less attention and effort at work but also poorer interactions with their team members and decreased achievement on tasks. In short, being lonely severely limited people's ability to focus, persevere, and collaborate. It sapped their grit.

There are two potential solutions to this problem. The first is to fundamentally reform how we define success — to view it in terms of social connections rather than individual achievement. In reality, though, this isn't going to happen, nor, in my opinion, should it. The human drive for discovery, mastery, and creation has led to amazing advancements in science, engineering, medicine, and the arts. It's as much a part of our DNA as is the desire to belong. The solution isn't to eschew individual achievement but to balance it with social connection. Using socially oriented emotions provides the answer. While directly helping us to achieve our personal goals, regularly practicing them will reduce our loneliness along the way by strengthening our ties to others, which will itself indirectly also bolster self-control. Put simply, these emotions offer a double shot when it comes to obtaining success.

7

Scaling Out
Reaching High Means Reaching Out

As we've just seen, the three prosocial emotions not only make us grittier, they make us more popular in an enduring way, which itself improves our perseverance and fortitude — the essential traits of grit. We've also glimpsed how contagious these emotions can be, and this chapter will examine that remarkable aspect in greater depth. Gratitude, compassion, and pride, when properly applied, can spread within our social networks, reinforcing their resilience.

Unlike cognitive mechanisms such as willpower, executive control, and habit formation, emotions aren't just inside our minds; they diffuse into the world. They're meant to influence not only our behavior toward others but also their behavior and actions toward us. Social emotions can be scaled outward; they can provide multiple routes by which to alter the behavior and success of larger groups. As we'll see, feeling and expressing gratitude, compassion, or pride not only significantly alters the emotional states of those around us, making them more supportive, conscientious, and diligent, but also lowers their levels of stress and enhances their well-being.

PYRAMID POWER

Pointy or well rounded? Anyone who has perused the literature on attaining success has no doubt seen these terms bandied about. It used to be the case that being well rounded — that is, good at lots of things — was the way to get into a top college, professional school, or the like. Play a sport? Have a solid GPA? Volunteer at a charitable organization? If you could check all those boxes, you were on your way. But as more and more people vied for the same number of slots, the criteria for standing out inevitably changed. Suddenly, it wasn't enough to play a sport, one had to excel in it. Working for a charity was fine but paled in comparison to starting one. With each passing year, the bar was being raised, requiring people to work harder and longer in order to compete. There was only one problem: the well rounded were running out of time.

Because there are only twenty-four hours in a day, the amount of effort we can expend is finite. So if we devote ourselves to becoming extremely good at one thing, we'll have less time to become good at other things. For this reason, the geometry of success had to change. People can only be so well rounded. When colleges and recruitment agencies had more well-rounded people than they knew what to do with, they began to identify attractive candidates in a different way: they searched for people with spikes.

If people's abilities were arrayed along several dimensions, the well rounded would look fairly uniform. They'd show decent levels of aptitude in any direction one looked; in essence, the profile of their strengths would be pretty flat. But the profiles of truly unique achievers — those with a single exceptional ability — would show a spike in a certain area that towered over their peers. So while they might not play sports *and* be in the glee club *and* have a strong GPA, some would have composed a symphony, or launched a startup, or discovered a supernova. In short, these spiky, or pointy, people will have shown dedication that fostered an exceptional, if somewhat one-dimensional, talent. These are the gritty people — the ones who have a passion to persevere toward an idiosyncratic and valued goal — and they are now held up as models for success. And I think this is mostly a good thing. Creativity, genius, and excellence do require exceptional devotion. It's the extremely rare person who, like Leonardo da Vinci, can display mastery in many realms. But that doesn't mean that most of us can't find an area in which we have something unique to offer if we possess the self-control to stay focused and engaged in our pursuit. What's more, outside the academic realm, well roundedness doesn't really matter that much. Rising in the ranks of a technology company depends on the ability to code or design in novel ways. Making it as an artist relies on developing creativity and technique.

Yet for all its benefits, pointiness has one significant drawback: geometrically speaking, spikes are about the least resilient shape in existence. Like a tower, a spike can soar to great heights, but faced with a disruption, it can easily tip and fall. The same logic applies to pointy people; when something goes wrong, they can fall farther than most, precisely because of the fragile path they took to reach their goals.

We don't always recognize this obvious danger, since the pointy among us have much going for them. Because of their initial successes, their future paths are partially eased; some potential bumps in the road have been removed, making them appear a bit more surefooted. For example, a person who achieves some kind of greatness in high school is more likely to get into a good university. And a person who graduates from a good university is more likely to land a job at a top firm because she is already a step ahead of others due to her school's reputation and the connections it's given her. Fair or not, doors will have been opened for her that would have remained closed for others no matter how hard they knocked. But when something does go wrong — when a top surgeon loses dexterity because of an accident, or a top executive gets unfairly passed over for the CEO slot she worked toward for years — the fall from the pinnacle can be devastating.

As I noted in the introduction, people who are gritty in terms of work ethic and self-discipline often suffer more in the face of adversity than do their peers. This fact suggests that the higher well-being associated with personality traits such as grit doesn't come from a greater ability to withstand failure but simply reflects lower rates of failure in general. In other words: people who fail less often are usually happier, but that doesn't mean that they're less likely to be hurt by failure if and when it comes.

So if a spike isn't a stable profile, what is? There must be a better way to reach high while also being resilient to disruptions. As it turns out, our ancestors found the solution: the pyramid. This shape maximizes height while maintaining resilience better than any other. While a relatively light hit can bring down a tower, it would take a much stronger one to tip a pyramid of the same height. In fact, the heights to which a pyramid can soar while still remaining stable are immense so long as the width of its base increases in kind.

If we once again move the motif from the physical realm to the human one, the implications easily translate: greater achievement requires a wider base. This base, however, can't simply be additional abilities, since any time and effort we put into developing one skill reduces the time and effort available to hone others. Either our core skill will suffer as a result, or our physical and psychological health will. That's what happens when we spread ourselves too thin. Fortunately, there's another, time-tested way to widen our base — social connection. As we've seen, cultivating gratitude, compassion, and pride reduces our own selfish desires for immediate gratification, nudging us to act in ways that make us a more attractive and valued spouse, parent, colleague, or friend. And unlike mastering skills, growing social connections isn't difficult. It doesn't take hours and hours day after day. All it requires is a willingness to connect, to share, to acknowledge the importance of others in our lives. Letting these emotions guide us provides an easy and, in truth, innate method for doing just that. We strengthen our foundations while simultaneously reaching for the sky.

Until now, I've primarily focused on the individual part — the ability of these emotions to shape a person's success and well-being. But using these emotions in social networks offers an added benefit: their contagious nature allows them to spread almost virally. As a person's base of support widens — as she regularly connects with more people — it will necessarily intersect with the bases of others, meaning that their emotions will spread back and forth in a reciprocal manner. One person's compassionate act will inspire gratitude in others. One person's pride in his team will inspire his peers to feel similarly. The result is a hallmark of resilient systems. As one part of the system encounters a problem, others work to right it. For example, when one person is tempted to throw in the towel on a project, the gratitude he might feel about help a colleague has given him can push him to persevere. As these moral feelings spread within the network, they will reinforce everyone's connections and self-control and, thereby, everyone's well-being and achievement. These emotions become a rising tide that lifts all boats.

A great example of this phenomenon can be seen in the effects compassion has on people who regularly confront burnout: health care workers. Wharton's Sigal Barsade, this time working with colleague Olivia O'Neill, examined what role compassion and social connection can play in the efforts and well-being of employees at long-term-care facilities. The two surveyed more than two hundred people working in different units within a large facility, collecting information on their performance as well as their feelings of social inclusion, empathy, and cooperation. Those who worked in units characterized by lower feelings of social attachment, trust, acceptance, and support — a composite the researchers labeled *companionate love* but which could easily be called empathy and compassion — showed not only poorer performance and engagement with the demanding work of patient care but also decreased satisfaction at work, more exhaustion, and greater absenteeism. The strength of these findings comes in recognizing that the work across the units Barsade and O'Neill examined was objectively the same. Tasks aren't more or less difficult or more or less boring on different floors of the same long-term-care facility. Yet simple differences in whether people felt connected to and empathy for those around them significantly increased their motivation and ability to complete the tasks at hand. Whenever one person felt overburdened and ready to give up, the emotional and actual support of others kept them going.

Pride works in a similar way. It enhances resilience while it builds skills. A wonderful example can be seen in an intervention study focused on a large group of Samoan teens living in San Francisco. These teens come from neighborhoods and families that often hover near the poverty line and, as a result, their prospects for academic and professional success can be limited. They also tend to be less tight-knit than those of other ethnicities and feel stigmatized by the stereotypes applied to them. To see what effect fostering pride in their group might have on the teens, a team of psychologists led by Christine Yeh created a program known as Wear Your Pride (WYP). The team expected that encouraging the teens to take pride in the traditions, strengths, and abilities of their cultural group might increase not only their drive to succeed but also their resilience and well-being. As part of the program, the teens spent time together learning about the cultural history of the Samoan people, its artistic achievements, its values and leaders. The main purpose was to help the students to build deeper connections with their group and feel greater pride in it while also learning artistic skills and working on a final project. At the end of the program, not only was pride increased but so were the teens' feelings of connection with their community and willingness to spend time honing their new skills. They also reported that taking part in the WYP program helped them draw support from and cooperate with their peers. One person's pride reinforced another's, and with it her persistence and sense of social connection.

Social emotions allow people to strive for the heights of achievement while also building a strong social base. Yes, it's true that feeling these emotions will divert some time away from individual pursuits, but it will be time well spent. Taking time to invest in others — to laugh with them, to happily surprise them, to comfort them — not only allows us to be more productive with the time we dedicate to work but also functions as a safety net in challenging times. It's also actually enjoyable in and of itself. Believe it or not, sacrificing to benefit others *does* make people happy; the human brain actually experiences it as rewarding. And what's rewarding tends to spread.

LONGING TO GIVE

Whatever else they might debate, everyone who studies self-control would agree that using willpower isn't fun. At best, it feels effortful; at worst, it's akin to root canal. This doesn't mean willpower isn't important or helpful but simply that it's not immediately reinforcing; you often have to force yourself to do it. Emotions such as gratitude, pride, and compassion work differently. Since they originated in social exchange, each, in its own way, pushes people to cooperate or share their expertise with others. Unlike willpower or habits, these emotions are intrinsically rewarding, meaning they tend to be self-perpetuating.

By definition, things that are rewarding usually bring happiness and satisfaction. But how much satisfaction any object or action will bring and how long it will last can vary a great deal. For two decades psychologists have been studying what makes us happy, and from that work a few basic principles have emerged. Yes, money does buy happiness, but only to a point. The lack of decent shelter, food, or medical care will likely cause stress and impede happiness. So depending on where a person lives, as costs of living differ dramatically by region, research shows that increasing incomes up to about $75,000 correspond to similar increases in feelings of well-being. Beyond that point, though, happiness relies on a different type of currency — one that involves interpersonal experiences.

Although a Rolex watch might bring a smile to many faces, that smile is unlikely to last as long as the one that comes from remembering the joys of playing catch with a child. It's just the way our minds are built. Nothing makes humans happier than the pleasant company of others. It's energizing and rewarding. The reason is no secret. Behaviors that are good for us in an evolutionary sense also *feel* good. That's how our minds get us to enact them. Sex is pleasurable because there's no greater evolutionary imperative than reproduction. The same with eating. Sweet and fatty foods taste so good because they contain lots of calories. (Such foods can endanger us now, of course, but recall that we evolved in a world of scarcity before the advent of junk food.) As important as food and sex are to our species's survival, cooperation and social support are not far behind. Consequently, we enjoy not only connecting with others but also the actions that cement those connections. And of those many actions, few are more helpful than giving.

Offering something of value to another is the essence of cooperation and is known to pay future dividends. By that metric, the
act of giving, all by itself, should, like sex or eating, feel pleasurable
even though in the moment it requires sacrifice. We've all heard it's
better to give than to receive, but until recently no one knew if the
human brain agreed with the sentiment. Finding out required psychologists Michael Norton and Elizabeth Dunn to design a clever
set of experiments.

Their first was quite straightforward. They asked a nationally
representative sample of Americans how much they engaged in
two types of spending: personal versus prosocial. Personal spending consisted of money used to buy gifts for themselves or to pay
bills and personal expenses. Prosocial spending consisted of gifts for
others or donations to charity. The subjects were also asked one additional question: "How happy do you feel in general?" The results
were clear. People who spent more of their money in prosocial ways
were happier — a pattern that held across all levels of income, dis-
proving the notion that the people who could devote more of their
wealth to others were happier just because they had more money in
general. Still, intriguing as these findings were, other reasons could
be put forward to explain them. More prosocially oriented people
might just be happier in general. If so, their spending patterns might
not be causing their happiness; they might just reflect something
that happy people tend to do.

To address this question, Dunn and Norton took a different
tack. On several mornings they approached people in public places
and asked them to report how happy they felt. Next, they did something none of these people expected. They handed them either $5
or $20 with one of two instructions: spend it on yourself today or
spend it on someone else. Later that evening the researchers con-
tacted each person and again asked them how happy they felt. As
before, giving money away proved more satisfying. Those who spent

their newfound cash on others were much happier at the end of the day than were those who bought something for themselves, regardless of their initial levels of happiness. Interestingly, how much they spent on others didn't matter; those who spent $5 weren't any less happy than those who spent $20. It was the act of giving itself that was satisfying.

While this finding might seem unambiguous, there was still the possibility that people were saying what they thought the experimenters wanted to hear. So just to be sure that the givers were reporting what they actually felt, as opposed to what they thought might be socially appropriate, others have looked a bit deeper into the brain. Using an MRI scanner, economist William Harbaugh and colleagues measured people's brain responses as they engaged in two types of giving: mandatory versus volitional. At the start of the session, Harbaugh gave each participant $100 while introducing them to a charitable organization focused on helping the hungry. He further explained that while in the scanner, they'd see proposed transfers of part of their $100 to the charity's account. Most times they'd be able to decide if they wanted the transaction to go through — a volitional decision. Other times, though, it would happen automatically, much like a mandatory tax. During each transaction, Harbaugh's team focused their scans on reward centers in the brain, where increasing activity reflects increasing pleasure. What they found supported Norton and Dunn's claims. Although the reward centers showed more activity with voluntary than with mandatory giving, they registered pleasure with either type. Giving of any kind made people feel happier.

Now, just as I've argued that cooperation can involve any type of resource, so too can its first step: giving. The pleasure giving brings need not be restricted to money. What psychologists call eudaimonic behaviors — activities whose rewards stem from social connection, empathy, gratitude, and the like — activate the same neurological reward centers in the brain as does any type of pleasurable reward, but unlike activation of these centers due to selfish pleasure seeking, prosocial activation is associated with a greater resistance to depression and loneliness over time. So as feelings of gratitude, compassion, and pride make us more likely to give to others, that giving itself is experienced as pleasurable, not as effort. It's a high that we want to experience again and again.

Viral Success

The feed-forward nature of emotion-based strategies makes them able to spread and amplify within a person over time. But they possess another feature that truly makes them a promising candidate to ensure success: they can spread virally. All emotions are contagious; they spread easily within groups. If those around you are happy, that joy can be infectious. If you're sad, the people you're with will feel the gloom. But socially oriented emotions, like the three I emphasize here, are special. Their contagion can take two forms: identical *and* reciprocal.

In identical contagion, one person's feelings are picked up and mirrored by another. Whether we realize it or not, our brains are constantly decoding the emotional cues expressed by those around us. And unless there's some reason to see these people as a threat, the mind will often adopt and embody those cues. For example, observing someone smile tends to trigger mirrored facial movements, albeit on a very small scale, in the observer. The same goes for almost any bodily motion we witness. This phenomenon — often referred to as nonconscious mimicry — is one mental mechanism designed to put us in synch with others. By copying their nonverbal cues, we tend to feel what they feel at a lower level, which helps our mind interpret their mental states. If I see someone else standing tall with her shoulders back and her head tilted up, I will likely adjust my body to mirror those cues in a subtle way, which my brain will then interpret as feeling proud. In other words, one way for me to know what someone else is feeling is to "try out" the cues they're giving off. And by so doing, I'll end up feeling a little bit of it myself.

Emotional contagion isn't limited to the nonverbal cues from others. It can travel via other means as well, and in large social networks it can influence feelings on a massive scale. One of the most convincing examples of this phenomenon comes from an experiment conducted by Facebook, wherein the company's data science team systematically altered the types of emotional content that appeared in more than 680,000 users' news feeds. For some users, they dialed back the number of positively toned posts they would see from their friends, while for others they dialed back negatively toned ones. In essence, they were manipulating the general tenor of the emotional expressions of people's virtual contacts or, put another way, the nature of the feelings people saw online. The results were unambiguous; people's moods moved toward the contents of their manipulated news feeds. Those who saw more sad posts subsequently posted more sad updates themselves. Those who saw more happy posts showed a similar mirroring. Even in the absence of face-to-face contact, people's minds picked up on emotional cues — here based on words — and spread those feelings through an essentially boundless network.

Similarly, when one person in a group feels grateful, proud, or compassionate, it will rub off a bit on those around her. It's actually a pretty familiar experience. Many people, for instance, commonly report feeling proud when standing next to someone with whom they're connected who is receiving recognition — a phenomenon known as basking in reflected glory. So if we look at ourselves as embedded in social networks, we will benefit not only from efforts to cultivate these three emotions on our own but also from others' efforts to do likewise. If there's a day when I'm just frustrated and annoyed, my ability to summon gratitude on my own will suffer, but encountering a grateful friend or colleague will give it a boost. I'll catch what I'm missing myself if there's enough of it around.

While catching emotions such as compassion, pride, and gratitude can only benefit us, those, of course, aren't the only emotions we feel. We also catch anger and dejection. Here again is why we have to think in terms of systems as opposed to individuals. In any connected system, it's true that contagious things — good or bad — can spread. But a resilient system can respond to negative disruptions and right itself. With respect to using emotional strategies, one easy way to do this is to ensure that enough "nodes" in the system — and by nodes I mean people — are feeling the "right" emotions. If they are, they will serve as a backstop against the spread of more destructive ones. Anger can't disperse too far if it encounters multiple instances of pride or compassion. And much like the response of the immune system to pathogens, problematic states will be excised.

The trick, of course, is to make sure that in any group the balance is correctly weighted. Tipping points are important. If too many emotional "pathogens" infect a group at once, the system might not be able to right itself. Avoiding that plight means paying attention to a group's culture. The norms have to be monitored and maintained. In the realm of cooperation, Yale psychologist David Rand has shown how slight changes in the baseline levels of honesty or dishonesty across a group can fundamentally alter how virtuously any single person in the group will behave. The same goes for emotions related to self-control. To bolster everyone's ability to achieve and persevere, baseline levels of the three target emotions need to remain elevated at the group level. That way, even though a few given people might have bad days now and again, there will be enough gratitude, compassion, and pride flowing throughout the system to compensate.

Although relying on the contagion of identical states (that is, gratitude begets gratitude) can be helpful in this effort, there is a second way. As I noted earlier, compassion, pride, and gratitude, due to their fundamental roles in social interaction, can spread, and thus be managed, in a reciprocal way. I could come to mirror my companion's feeling in a passive way, through observation. But alternatively, I might be made to feel a different state because of how my companion acts toward me. For example, as we saw earlier, if I'm feeling compassion, I'm more likely to help someone. That kind act will likely do more than just help him out of a jam. It will change how he *feels*, too. He'll feel grateful, and that gratitude will make him more likely to reach out to help someone else. These newly induced emotional states can't help but feed forward, shaping the next round of behavior: compassion begets gratitude, which subsequently leads to a helpful action, which begets compassion in another. After all, this is the very purpose of these emotions; they evolved to keep social exchange moving. And as these states pass reciprocally among us, they will also increase everyone's self-control, diligence, focus, mental fortitude, and resilience.

While I could point to many examples of this phenomenon, one of my favorites comes from a study done by Wharton's Adam Grant and Harvard's Francesca Gino, who examined perseverance in an environment that is rife with rejection: fundraising. Over a two-week period, Grant and Gino recorded the number of calls fundraisers made to solicit donations for a university. Between the first and second week, however, half of the fundraisers received a visit from the university's director of annual giving. During that visit, the director expressed her appreciation for their work. To get a sense of how this expression of gratitude affected the fundraisers, Gino and Grant had them report how valued and appreciated they felt by their superiors.

What happened during the following week was remarkable. Whereas the average performance of both groups — those who heard from the university official and those who didn't — had been virtually the same during the first week of the study, those who had heard the grateful message upped their fundraising efforts by 50 percent during the second week. What's important here is that the fundraisers weren't feeling grateful themselves, but rather feeling valued and proud. One person's gratitude stoked another's pride and bolstered that second person's efforts and fortitude on a difficult task that is often met with rude rejection.

Adding support for this view, Grant, this time in collaboration with Yale School of Management professor Amy Wrzesniewski, has demonstrated that merely anticipating gratitude can increase success. Specifically, they showed that among a set of employees, those who anticipated receiving gratitude for their work, and thus who also anticipated their own coming feelings of pride, performed better than employees who were not anticipating either emotion. This increased performance can of course help ensure that the thanks and pride the employees anticipated will come to pass, which in turn will motivate additional dedication on their part and subsequent gratitude from their superiors. And on it goes — an emotion-driven, communal, upward spiral of success.

One of the best ways to facilitate this spiral is not only increasing how often we feel gratitude, compassion, and pride but also being willing to show those feelings to others, even those to whom they're not directed. Reciprocal contagion — the kind where we might lead a person to feel grateful for the compassion we show her — will take care of itself as we cultivate these three emotions in our own lives. As we feel them more, we'll behave in accord. Identical contagion, however, can be boosted by increasing the signal relative to the noise. For example, unless a person's gratitude is directed toward me, I might not really know that he's feeling it. The cues to his emotional state can be easy to overlook. However, if he's open about them — if he expresses gratitude publicly or tells people what he's feeling — the strength of the signal grows. And as emotions become easier to see, they become easier to catch.

Within the contexts of groups, this strategy also suggests that leaders and managers work to instill a culture that encourages honest expression and sharing of these emotions. To the extent that members of a team or classroom believe that showing gratitude, compassion, and authentic pride is valued, any attempts to inhibit public displays of them will lessen the contagion. And if the spread of these states occurs on a big enough scale — a societal one — it could help begin to solve some very large and thorny issues. We'll examine that possibility in the next chapter.

Scaling Up

Stimulating Societal Success

Until now, we've been examining self-control and success under a microscope of sorts. We've seen how gratitude, compassion, and pride make people more future-oriented, and thus more willing to control their impulses and persevere toward their goals. We've seen how these states simultaneously buffer people's minds and bodies in the face of the daily stresses we call life. And we've seen how these emotions can flow through and reinforce social networks, making the individuals who compose them happier and more resilient. But there's another benefit of adopting an emotional route to success: it can scale up as well as out.

By scaling up, I mean these emotions can shape decisions that improve society as a whole. Climate change, crumbling infrastructure, health care, and similar vexing problems are all dilemmas of intertemporal choice: part of their solution requires accepting costs in the short term to pave the way for a better future. But solving these problems is especially challenging because it can be so diffi-cult to connect palpable sacrifices we must make in the short term with future benefits that will likely be minuscule (if not invisible) to us as individuals.

WHEN MORE MINDS ARE WORSE THAN ONE

How much is the public good worth? It can be a touchy question. Although no one in their right mind wants others to suffer, offer-ing them assistance takes money and effort. Add to this fact that any one person is also part of this "public" — each of us as citizens of a society benefit to some extent because of the taxes, efforts, and re-lated resources contributed by other people — and the equation can become quite complex. It takes the notion of individuals in quid pro quo cooperation to a much larger scale. Yet it's a scale that, whether we realize it or not, we play a part in every day. Whom we vote for, what policies we support, and how we consume resources all play a role in determining not only our own outcomes but everyone else's.

To study how people decide what tradeoffs are acceptable when it comes to individual versus public gains and losses, behavioral economists have created an experimental game that elegantly cap-tures the issues involved. It's called the public-goods game, and as its name suggests, it gives people the option of contributing their money to a public pot or keeping it for themselves. To simulate the benefits one receives from contributions to society, the money placed in the public pot is multiplied by a factor and the resulting profits are then distributed among all the players. There are two catches, though. The first is that the factor by which the public pot is multiplied is always less than the number of players, which means the money any player will receive back from the public pot is less than the amount she would possess if she kept her money. This sets up a dynamic where the highest profits for the group occur if everyone contributes fully, but the greatest profits for individuals come if they're free riders who profit off the contributions of others. The second is that decisions are usually secret; no one knows whether any given person decided to contribute to the public good.

In many ways, this situation mirrors the dynamics of daily life. Unless people declare their contributions or positions, we don't know who's paying what in taxes, who or what policies they voted for, if they're relying on public assistance for support when they might easily get a job, if they're paying more for clean energy, and so forth. The theory behind taxes, many social policies, tithing, and the like is that each person contributes some of his individual resources (adjusted for his station in life) to ensure benefit for all. But as we know, the system never works as equitably as it should.

For game theorists, the best strategy to use in such situations is clear. If what you truly care about is maximizing profits, be a free rider. Don't give anything. Yet in the public-goods game, a different trajectory typically emerges. At first most people contribute a fair amount to the public pot — typically leaving economists banging their heads, as it seems quite irrational. This behavior stems from our innate intuitions. Historically speaking, when people lived in small groups and shared resources — land for farming or grazing, joint efforts at hunting — free riding was costly. Unless a person had complete anonymity, the shadow of the future always lurked. Sure, a person might come out ahead in the short run, but as others realized he wasn't contributing anything, he'd be punished, ostracized, or worse. So even today, as people begin to play a public-goods game, they feel obliged to act communally. In a game where true anonymity is the rule, however, people begin to realize that selfish behavior won't lead to any long-term costs to their reputation. So as the game progresses, and people get a sense that not everyone might be paying their fair share, contributions shrink until, at the end, there are only a few dedicated "givers" who insist on doing the right thing.

What we're seeing in this game is a type of expanded prisoner's dilemma, one where people's outcomes are tied not directly to the actions of a partner but rather to the actions of a larger group. The result is a diffusion of responsibility combined with a greater uncertainty that rewards will be realized. And so, for many, it becomes easier to be selfish. If there are free riders who aren't being punished, it's tempting to become one of them. After all, they're not only benefiting in the moment, they're making it more unlikely that your sacrifices will be rewarded in the long run.

Reasoning like this, combined with our usual preference for immediate gratification, can make national or global problems extremely difficult to address. Let's take climate change. A poll from 2015 conducted by the *New York Times* in collaboration with Stanford University and the nonpartisan environmental research group Resources for the Future found that an overwhelming majority of Americans (including half of those who identify as Republicans) believe global warming is a problem and, in theory, support government action to deal with it. Yet many also note that there are economic costs to doing so, which, as we can see given the slow pace with which climate change is being addressed, limits people's enthusiasm for dealing with the problem.

Over time the benefits of addressing climate change will surely outweigh the immediate costs, but those benefits won't be realized for decades. And the people who realize them will likely not be those who accept the most sacrifice. The Appalachian coal miners who might lose their jobs won't likely see as much benefit as people living in low-lying coastal cities where rising sea levels will be a problem. This widely distributed nature of rewards leads people to discount the future to an even greater degree than usual.

We can see something similar regarding infrastructure. To put it bluntly, the United States is crumbling from the inside out. In 2007 the Federal Highway Administration found that over 25 percent of bridges in the United States were structurally deficient. In 2008 the Association of State Dam Safety Officials estimated that more than four thousand dams were unsafe or deficient in important ways. In fact, in 2010 it was estimated that needed expenditures for U.S. infrastructure improvements — ranging from drinking water systems to roads and schools — would fall short by more than $1.8 trillion. Logically, it seems unthinkable that voters and politicians would let this happen. And while it's certainly true that throwing money at problems isn't always the answer, as there needs to be accountability for how a government's money is spent, it's just as true that money must be spent to keep infrastructure in a good state of repair. Yet, given the crumbling state of things in the United States and in many other countries, there's no question that those funds aren't being spent. A big reason for the consistent shortfall comes, as one might now expect, from the usual human tendency to discount the future. Most people would rather go on an extra trip this weekend than devote that money to unspecified bridge repairs. But as I noted above, the discounting that gives rise to this phenomenon is exacerbated at the societal level by the very low likelihood, statistically speaking, that any given individual will be on a given bridge when it falls.

This simple fact can lead to poor policy decisions just as readily as it can individual decisions. Cornell economist Robert Frank offered an insightful example. During the last U.S. recession, people were focused on saving money at all costs. Yet Frank eloquently argued that deferring maintenance on infrastructure, while feeling like it's saving money, can do just the opposite. As he pointed out in a 2010 column for the *New York Times,* the Nevada Department of Transportation estimated that rehabilitating a ten-mile section of Interstate 80 would cost about $6 million. Delaying it for two years, however, would raise the cost to $30 million, due to continued deterioration. For this project, and many like it, spending more money at the time — investing in the future — would actually be a bargain. During the recession, Frank correctly noted, labor and material costs were at remarkably low levels due to high unemployment and excess capacity. It would never be cheaper to build than it was at that moment. Nonetheless, additional economic stimulus packages were mostly foresworn. People felt that *their* future was uncertain, and so they, and the politicians they supported, focused on the present — preserving *their* resources in the moment — at the cost of larger gains that would have been realized and shared by all down the line.

In many ways, the more minds that are involved, the harder it becomes to get people to do the right thing. The more chances there are for free riding — for people not to pay their share — the more difficult it is for other people to believe they themselves will benefit and aren't being played for suckers. While a strong argument can be made statistically for contributing to the common "pot" — we all benefit from sound roads and bridges, reliable agriculture, clean air and water, a strong military — those communally supported benefits can feel abstract, very removed from daily life. Whereas historically the sacrifice, self-control, and cooperation needed to survive took place among relatively small groups of people who could, in many ways, hold one another accountable, they now depend on millions often separated by great distances. As a result, we rarely recognize the benefits we receive from other people's contributions until we're in a very vulnerable situation.

Solving these problems requires self-control on a massive scale. So, too, does addressing the associated problem of taking too much of a publicly available resource for selfish purposes. This phenomenon — known as the tragedy of the commons — occurs when people deplete shared resources for immediate gain. For example, if fishermen overfish to make individual profits in the short term, fish stocks that feed everyone will decline and, over time, could disappear completely.

Situations where appreciating gains requires complex, statistical thinking *and* contact with those who are harmed by selfish decisions constitute a toxic environment for exerting executive control. The mental gymnastics required to reason out and appreciate why self-control is necessary or right become more arduous. We need an approach that can move people on a very basic, intuitive level. One that doesn't require elaborate thinking. One that can readily take the mind's ancestral methods of solving problems of cooperation and self-control on a smaller scale and amplify them to work on larger ones: social emotions.

EMOTIONAL MORES

The three emotions touted in this book possess two common traits that affect how people form or change their attitudes and beliefs. First, as we've seen, they combat our tendency to discount the value of future rewards. Second, they alter our perceptions of other people so that we believe they're more likely to be cooperative and trustworthy. Taken together, morally toned emotions such as gratitude, compassion, and pride seem especially apt to change attitudes in ways that benefit everyone in the long run. By making us all more future-oriented and less suspicious of potential free riding, they ease the path to contributing or sacrificing to enhance the long-term greater good.

Let me provide some proof. One important way in which the views of environmental policies by liberals and conservatives differ is that, for liberals, issues such as climate change, recycling, and species conservation are perceived to be moral ones. They invoke moral feelings when they're being considered. Liberals are proud of recycling.

They're compassionate toward the species that will suffer from environmental harm. Now, if we add to this difference the truism that people tend to be more willing to accept short-term costs for a goal when they're feeling morally involved in an issue, the tendency of liberals to favor environment-friendly policies would make good sense. To them, the cost is worth it, partly because their moral emotions prevent them from primarily focusing on immediate gains.

If this view is correct, it should be possible to alter conservatives' attitudes toward environmental policies by rousing moral emotions within them and linking these states to a relevant cause. Fortunately, Stanford sociologist Robb Willer, along with University of Toronto psychologist Matthew Feinberg, examined just this possibility. They designed a morality-based pro-environmental message, but rather than couch it in terms of the moral principle of "do no harm" — the way liberal environmentalists typically do — they framed it in terms of the moral principle of purity. The focus on purity stems from decades of research showing that conservatives view purity as much more morally important than do liberals, suggesting that they're more likely to be grateful for and appreciate things in untarnished conditions. The corresponding environmental message encouraged people to protect natural habitats from "desecration" so that future generations could experience the "uncontaminated purity and value of nature."

Willer and Feinberg had self-identified conservatives read this purity-framed environmental appeal or a more typical "do no harm" one. The conservatives who'd read the purity version reported more positive attitudes toward legislation meant to protect the environment than did those who read the other version. In fact, the conservatives who read the purity-toned message ended up also reporting a greater belief in global warming even though information on climate change was not included in the original message. Here, in particular, we can see the contagious effect of moral emotions on perceptions and decisions about the future.

Okay, fine. It seems clear that when moral emotions are evoked, people will *say* they value decisions and behaviors that are in the communal long-term interest. But when push comes to shove — when people are facing real costs or inconveniences — will their words match their deeds? We need answers to this question before we start using moral emotions to try to change society. I'm happy to report that early answers are quite encouraging.

One example comes from electricity use. In many metropolitan areas, electricity is delivered through an aging infrastructure — the power grid — that is too often overtaxed on hot summer days when people seek the comfort of a cool home or office. In 2013 alone, major blackouts due to high demand left hundreds of thousands without power in New York, Washington, Philadelphia, and Boston. Similarly major outages occurred in Canada, Japan, and India. Blackouts like these are, in fact, quite avoidable; power utilities have had the technology to prevent them for years. The problem is customers — or more specifically, their lack of self-control.

At heart, the dynamics of summer blackouts constitute a public-goods dilemma. As in the tragedy of the commons, there's a resource that benefits many, but it remains viable only if no one hogs it. If too many people take too much of it, it becomes depleted or, in this case, broken as the electrical circuits short. The easy way to solve this problem, of course, is for people to cooperate. Each person needs to use self-restraint to consume less of the resource than she would like, which in this case means accepting a home or office temperature that is a little warmer than ideal. The alternative is for everyone to turn their air conditioners on max and risk the possibility that power will temporarily disappear and everyone will suffer more.

As might be expected given what we know about self-control, most people set their thermostats to cooler temperatures than what might be best for the energy grid either because they hope to profit from other people's sacrifices or because they don't want to be a sucker and enable other people's selfish behavior. In an effort to try to nudge cooperative behavior, many utilities regularly offer to install small radio devices near their customers' air conditioners that can receive a signal when the risk of a blackout is high. When such a signal is received, these devices automatically raise the thermostat's temperature a few degrees, thereby reducing the tax on the power grid. It's quick, it's easy, yet very few people agree to have the device installed. In communities around the country, participation almost never breaks 20 percent.

A big reason for such poor compliance rates, as I suggested before, comes from the fact that we're now dealing with situations that dramatically differ in terms of scale and technology from the ones in which humans evolved. Historically speaking, it was pretty easy to know if someone was taking more than their share of a resource. If a person let his cows graze too much on the public meadow, drew too much water from the public well, or didn't help with the local barn raising, others would likely notice. But when we're talking about a scale of thousands of people and behaviors that are easy to conceal, like setting a thermostat inside your own home, the usual mechanisms that might constrain selfish behavior become easier to suppress or ignore. If no one knows a person is being selfish, he's less likely to worry about tarnishing his reputation. And if some people are less likely to worry about their reputations, others will also become less likely to use self-control to behave in cooperative and admirable ways.

As intractable as this dilemma might seem, there are fairly simple ways to address it. If technology and scale allow people to hide their selfishness, all that's needed to change their behavior is making it public. One of the most powerful examples of this comes from an ingenious study led by Harvard economist Erez Yoeli in collaboration with PG&E, one of the largest utility companies in the United States. PG&E, with quite limited success, had been offering customers $25 to sign up to have a blackout device hooked up to their air conditioners. Yoeli's team wondered whether the utility might have better luck if, rather than incentivizing people with a privately received reward, it chose to tap into its customers' concerns about how others saw them. So a small change was made in the way people could sign up to have a blackout device installed. While customers continued to receive the same invitation to participate in the mail, they would now sign up by writing their name on a form that was posted in a public place for their neighbors to see. This way, everyone would know who agreed to have a device installed in their home. And since these devices automatically set cooling temperatures, people could be pretty certain that those who signed up weren't cheating behind closed doors. Of course, this also meant that it was equally easy to determine who was likely behaving selfishly. Those who signed up could feel pride; those who didn't would likely feel nothing but a cold shoulder from their neighbors.

The results were impressive: participation in the blackout prevention program more than tripled. Even better, this new strategy was cost effective for the utility. Yoeli's team calculated that PG&E would have had to increase the money they offered people to enroll in the program by $145 each in order to get a similar rate of compliance. Think about that. A few sheets of paper versus $170 per person to achieve the same positive outcome. It's a no-brainer. Pride is a powerful tool for self-restraint, and the effect of public sign-up sheets was most pronounced under conditions where people were more likely to regularly interact with their neighbors, and thus have the effects of pride spread and be socially reinforced. For example, the effect was stronger in high-rise apartment buildings where everyone could easily see the list of names in the lobby. Similarly, it was more effective for homeowners than for renters, as the latter were likely to be less invested in their community for the long run.

Taken together, findings like these suggest that to the extent a populace encourages and enables moral emotions among its members, the likelihood that its general outlook will be a forward-looking one increases. There are two complementary ways to do this, of course. One is to embed these states in a cultural ethos — to make them a central part of the norms a society values so that children come to internalize them as they grow up. The compassionate, for instance, can't help but want to act in ways that benefit others even at some immediate cost to themselves.

One of the best examples of this strategy can be seen in Denmark. The Danes believe that learning empathy and compassion is as essential for future success and happiness as is learning math or literature. And it's a view backed by solid research. That's why Danish schools often incorporate empathy lessons and exercises as part of their regular curriculum. By teaching kids how to mentally put themselves in others' shoes, to work cooperatively, and to support one another when needed, the students enter adulthood with a greater desire and ability to act compassionately. And while there isn't an experiment that directly ties this enhanced compassion to other aspects of Danish society, potential links are obvious to see. Not only do the Danes habitually rank near the top of the happiest societies on earth, but more to the point here, they also rank near the top for advocating forward-looking environmental policies. For example, the people of Denmark have embraced tax policies that encourage both lower energy use and the development of new, green technologies. Both of these, of course, require people to contribute more money in the present in the form of taxes but offer the potential for greater shared gains in years to come.

A second way to use social emotions to foster a society's long-term success is to frame policies or actions in ways that evoke moral emotions and concerns. After all, one reason people spend more for a hybrid car is the pride they take in showing not only that they can afford it but also that they're doing their part for the environment. To the degree, then, that societal issues of pressing concern can honestly be framed in moral terms, doing so will offer increased persuasive power as long — and this point cannot be overemphasized — as the people empowered to make choices share the same moral code. As Willer and Feinberg's work shows, sometimes making an issue seem morally relevant requires tailoring the message to a group's existing moral tenets (such as "purity"). Nonetheless, if people become willing to feel gratitude, compassion, and pride in response to a problem, they'll also become more willing to sacrifice to solve it. And as more and more people do so, the average level of self-control and cooperation in a society will spiral upward as expectations for getting suckered by anonymous free riders diminishes.

Still, as powerful as emotions can be in guiding decisions, it's important to recognize that people usually bring a good deal of previous knowledge — whether accurate or not — to debates about the laws and policies that affect them. This information will necessarily play a role in shaping their ultimate decisions. Given this, I want to point out one additional benefit that can come from weaving social emotions into a society's fabric: they help prevent us from blinding ourselves to facts. As we saw in the experiment on cheating I described in chapter 2, the human mind is, at times, more than willing to twist facts and views in a self-interested way; people were quite ready to see their own transgressions as less objectionable than they truly were. It should come as no surprise, then, that the conscious mind will do just the same when it comes to facts that can get in the way of our more immediate desires. We can too easily be tempted to believe "fake news" when it suits our purposes.

One of the clearest examples of this bias can be seen in work showing how short-term economic worries directly alter which facts people can recall, and thus believe, about the role humans play in climate change. In a clever experiment conducted at New York University, the psychologists Erin Hennes, John Jost, and colleagues invited more than two hundred people to hear and evaluate a podcast and a video. The podcast, which they heard first, was economic in theme and purportedly discussed the current financial outlook for the United States. There were two versions of the specially created podcast, and while they drew on the same facts, one version indicated that the United States remained in an economic recession, while the other said the U.S. economy was in recovery. After listening to one version or the other, everyone watched a six-minute NASA video that presented evidence for human-caused climate change. A few minutes after watching the video, people were queried, without any forewarning, about specific facts contained in the video.

The results confirmed that people's economic insecurity significantly altered their memories for the facts presented in the video. Those who saw the recession-themed version and were more concerned about their present earning power systematically misremembered facts in a way that made climate change seem to be less of a threat. As one example, they consistently reported the decline of summer sea ice in the Arctic to be smaller than reported in the video. It wasn't that they had a poorer memory; that would have resulted in as many overestimates as underestimates. No, their minds were skillfully and intentionally fudging the numbers in a way that made them feel freer to ignore long-term consequences in favor of immediate benefits — a pattern that was magnified among those who most strongly endorsed a belief that the current U.S. economic system is fair.

This research highlights a profound and very worrisome obstacle. Rational analysis won't foster self-restraint if the "rational" mind massages the facts. After all, there's no reason for people to accept sacrifices now if the future doesn't present any real challenges. And toward that end, we've seen that our minds harbor a motive to whitewash any facts that threaten our ability to obtain more pleasure or satisfaction in the short run, even and including when that means wiping our memories a bit. Yet, as we also saw earlier, choosing to focus on our emotional responses to quandaries can provide an antidote of sorts to motives for immediate satisfaction — irrespective of whether those motives target decisions that involve only us or ones whose ramifications are to be felt on a much larger scale.

The message here is clear: a society that carefully cultivates and targets gratitude, compassion, and pride is likely to be more amenable to conserving its resources and building toward the future. The best way to help a society move in that direction, however, isn't so obvious. While tailoring messages to focus on moral themes, as Willer and Feinberg demonstrated, offers one effective route to bring these emotions online for people when they consider policies, its success depends on exposing them to appeals that are carefully crafted to be useful on an issue-by-issue basis. The same goes for strategies like the public postings Yoeli used. A more robust method would increase how often people regularly feel these states, as it would constantly prepare their minds to favor future benefits for all over present pleasures for the self. And here, I think, the Danes are wise to focus on social emotions in their school curricula.

In the United States, the idea of teaching emotional intelligence (EI), both in schools and in corporate training programs, has been quite popular. But in the typical way it's taught an important foundational element is often neglected. Instructors and trainers focus on teaching people how to read the emotions of others and how to calm their own. The aim is to be able to predict what another feels — which can be used strategically to manipulate or interact with them — and to keep one's own emotions regulated so that little Johnny (or big Johnny) doesn't cause any disruptions at work or school and remains focused. But there's a third part to EI that almost never gets talked about: how to use emotions as tools to achieve ends. It's here that we should focus our efforts as a society. Much as the Danes teach the importance of empathy and compassion to achieve successful and harmonious ends, we should teach people in the United States and other countries how to regularly cultivate and call upon gratitude, compassion, and authentic pride. The exact strategies used can vary by age and venue — from storytelling and modeling for the young to specific exercises and tactics (like those mentioned earlier in this book) for adults.

The goal here is to start as early as possible to offer examples of how to use social emotional responses successfully. This is something that institutions as well as parents can do. I'm not arguing that ideas about what they should feel should be rammed down people's throats. Rather, I'm suggesting that simply teaching the value of moral emotions — through both verbal instruction and modeling — can foster virtuous norms. Our minds come seeded with these emotional mechanisms; those seeds just need to be tended so that they can blossom.

CODA

As I close, I hope I've made the case not only that the ability to be future-oriented, to resist immediate gratification, is essential to long-term success but also that using, not ignoring or suppressing, certain emotions offers a better route to attaining long-term goals. It's not that executive function and its cognitive minions are always problematic; willpower, reasoning, planning, and the like certainly have a role to play. However, we need to consider the proper size of that role in light of their limitations. As we've seen, they're often biased, relatively weak, and exhausting or even harmful to maintain.

Finding ways to embrace the emotions of gratitude, compassion, and pride in your life can bring multifaceted benefits. Yet for all the gains these social emotions offer when it comes to reinforcing success, combating loneliness, and improving health, it's important to recognize that they're not just a luxury to be wielded by those who have the inclination and expertise to do so. The world of work is quickly changing and with it the skills necessary to excel.

In many ways, we may be approaching an inflection point of sorts — one where the skills and strategies that have served people well in the professional arena are losing their efficacy. Staying ahead of the curve will likely require us to reconsider the nature and importance of social- and emotion-based capacities, not only for reaching our own goals and maximizing well-being but for navigating the changing dynamics of work in the twenty-first century.

THE CHANGING WORLD OF WORK

As we move into a working environment shaped more and more by new technologies and social media, the skills people need to succeed, and even the ways in which they interact, are rapidly changing. As a result, the abilities that underlie success and leadership — skills related to empathy, cooperation, creativity, and communication — are rising in importance. As *New York Times* reporter Claire Cain Miller noted in a popular 2015 piece, the only occupations that have shown consistent growth in wages and opportunities since 2000 are those requiring both social and cognitive skills. Other jobs — the ones that require only technical expertise or completion of repetitive tasks — are being economically devalued as advances in technology allow them to become automatized. Machines can do repetitive and highly intricate tasks more quickly, for longer, and more accurately than can any human. Still, machines have limits: they lack empathy and a moral sense. They can't figure out if someone is confused or upset, nor can they help people work through interpersonal conflicts or learn how and when to be a good listener or friend. These abilities remain the province of the human mind and likely will for decades to come.

In the workplace, what now gives a person an edge is the ability to build and maintain relationships with colleagues and clients. And doing so requires a capacity not only to understand what others are thinking and feeling but also to extend compassion, gratitude, and fairness toward them. As we've seen, a coworker, instructor, or manager who is emotionally in touch, welcoming, and principled can bring out the best in not just herself but in her team. And having more employees with these qualities both lowers the stress and increases the happiness of workers as well as, in doing so, raises the bottom line. When employees cooperate with and support one another, the organization itself becomes more creative, resilient, and forward-looking. Everyone's dedication increases as gratitude, compassion, and pride flow through their social networks in reciprocal ways.

Some solid evidence for this view comes from a study conducted at Google in 2009. The People Operations Department (POD) — Google's term for human resources — had the search-engine behemoth turn its lens inward to gather and analyze information about the performance of its own managers and teams. The POD scoured employees' performance reviews, awards, feedback surveys, and the like for all types of descriptive words and phrases. Once they had these terms, they looked at how they correlated with measures of productivity and achievement. While many Google employees initially expected that technical expertise would be the quality in a team manager that mattered most for a work group's success, it actually came in last among the eight factors identified as important by the POD project team. The two qualities in a manager that best predicted her team's achievement were (1) a supportive and caring demeanor — for example, making time for one-on-one meetings and helping coworkers solve problems — and (2) being results oriented. Yes, technical know-how offered a boon, but brilliant managers who possessed it without also having a cooperative, empathic, emotional side ended up creating a less constructive and productive

environment. Their teams suffered, professionally and psychologically. Findings like these are leading many star CEOs such as Micro-
soft's Satya Nadella, Slack's Stewart Butterfield, and Zappos' Tony
Hsieh to have their companies value qualities such as empathy and
kindness when it comes to recruiting employees and creating corporate culture.

Yet another way that the world of work is changing has to do
with the importance of creativity and the ways that a culture of
impatience can hinder it. Policy wonks may recognize the term
NIMTO, which in Washington-speak stands for *not in my term of
office* and implies that while an idea may be good in the long term,
no politician wanting to get reelected will embrace it if it causes
short-term sacrifices that could be used against him by an oppo-
nent. The typical thinking goes like this: sure, the roads need fixing,
and that requires raising revenue, but let the next Congress figure
that out, as asking people to pay more in taxes would be a blight on
my record. In business the problem is much the same. You might
call it NIMFY: *not in my fiscal year.* Over the past two decades companies, like politicians, have increasingly been making decisions
focused primarily on the short term. They didn't want to take a
chance that they'd disappoint the Street with their next earnings report, and when the need to report sunny annual profits rises to the
fore, long-term planning and investing quickly fall by the wayside.
Almost everyone, almost everywhere, has been focused on locking
in a gain in the here and now, future be damned.

As we've seen already, the problems that can arise from this bias
toward the present are many. But what's becoming ever more certain is that there's an additional one: a decrease in innovation. Innovation requires creativity. And as Harvard's Teresa Amabile has
shown, creativity requires freedom to explore and fail. And freedom to explore and fail requires a lack of stress to meet an impend-
ing deadline. The upshot is that a focus on the present limits future

potential in almost any area. A quick look at which companies have been the most innovative over the past decade or so proves the point. Google, Facebook, and Amazon are clear examples. These and several other denizens of Silicon Valley made a point of not focusing on immediate profit. They warned investors not to expect rosy budget sheets during the early days. Corporations such as these recognized that to be creative — to design and develop something truly innovative — requires long-term effort and the freedom from the obligation to provide immediate rewards to impatient investors.

We're now beginning to see this idea spread to other, more traditional sectors of the corporate world. In 2015, Toyota launched a new type of stock meant to combat short-termerism. Its Model AA shares, named after its first model of passenger car, are sold at a premium over its common stock and cannot be traded for at least five years. The shares do, however, come with a guarantee that they can be sold back at the issue price as a minimum. This new type of stock constitutes an effort to give Toyota a more stable investor base, one that will allow it the time and ensured liquidity necessary to pursue innovative research and development projects whose payoffs might be years in the future. This trend is likely to grow, and it rewards the type of thinking that social emotions encourage — a willingness to sacrifice or strive in the short term in pursuit of better future outcomes. Working to instill or evoke these emotions in colleagues, peers, or customers using the techniques I've described will help alter the impatience for rewards that can sabotage the space and support necessary for personal and corporate innovation.

Yet, sadly, our education system doesn't teach the mechanics or the benefits of long-term thinking. As Miller noted in her article, aptly titled "Why What You Learned in Preschool Is Crucial at Work," the skills that matter for success now are centered on social virtues: how to cooperate, how to be fair, how to take another's perspective, how to be patient. But once kids move from preschool to the upper grades and college, the model of learning rapidly changes from one where students typically work in several small groups where negotiation is important to one characterized by more isolating pursuits such as note taking, studying for exams through memorization, and writing individual papers. If the modern office emulated this environment, that might make some sense. The problem, of course, is that it doesn't. The current workplace is coming more and more to resemble preschool life in its dynamics. The jobs and companies that offer more opportunities are the ones that will require and value social and emotional adroitness. People have to be able to function in malleable small groups, cooperate at solving problems, trust one another, and manage different interpersonal priorities and concerns. Prospering here requires people skills, not solely working to solve a task or to reach a goal in isolation.

The trust and feelings of support that come with a working environment rich in these social emotions also directly benefit creativity. The current model of grit — one that uses executive function to focus attention and perseverance at all costs — can diminish mental flexibility. In a series of experiments conducted by Gale Lucas and colleagues at the University of Southern California, people high in grit were more likely to persist in using failing strategies to complete a task. They'd double down in an effort to prove that their chosen strategy to solve problems or to win a game was the right one even as it became clear that it was going nowhere. An environment that fosters perseverance based on enhancing empathy and trust, however, will do the opposite. Believing that you can depend on your colleagues, that you can trust them not to disparage you for making a bad choice, is central to fostering creativity.

In more ways than one, we're approaching a tipping point. As people try to climb the ladder of success, more and more of them are staring out over an abyss of loneliness and frustration. As they rely on rationality and cognitive "tricks" to give them the self-control necessary to remain focused on the future, they're being simultaneously weighed down and held back by the stresses and efforts entailed in doing so while also producing quick results. And as they strive to become even more focused by ignoring their emotional lives and skills, they're not only limiting their abilities but also fraying the social fabric that for millennia has been our species's source of resilience and achievement. If, as a society, we keep following this path in our attempts to reach the pinnacle of success, we're ultimately going to tip toward failure — a reality that many corporate leaders are beginning to recognize. The human mind and body didn't evolve to work in an ascetic, socially isolating way. We'll never be as good (or as happy) at being a cog as will a computer or a robot. Solving the problem — helping people to flourish — will require not just helping them to value the future over the present but doing so in a way that simultaneously builds the traits that matter for working with others. In short, it will build character.

CONSTRUCTING CHARACTER

As I've shown, there are two routes to building self-control. One is top down, requiring constant cognitive vigilance to overcome temptations and correct behavior. The other is bottom up, requiring the simple feeling of specific emotions. When we evoke these most basic building blocks of virtue — compassion, gratitude, and pride — self-control, along with other social virtues, automatically blossoms. And in many ways, this offers a key insight into how we psychologically grow. Using these emotions builds not only self-control but also many other qualities that draw others to us.

Throughout this book we've seen time and again how experiencing one of these emotions alters the mind's responses and, therefore, people's decisions and behaviors. Gratitude, which itself is often considered a virtue, enhances self-control and, if experienced regularly, perseverance. It increases honesty and trustworthy behavior. It also leads people to be more generous and loyal. Compassion does much the same, while also providing a sense of purpose and efficacy, a belief that people can make a difference. Pride, too, has been shown to increase motivation and diligence, while also making it more likely that people will approach challenging tasks with zeal and be admired for so doing.

What I'm saying, in essence, is that by cultivating these emotions, we will be planting the seeds for other virtues to grow. These three emotions are the engines of character. They boost self-control and related traits that, together, contribute to the development of a person ready to meet whatever obstacles life puts in the way. And as a result, using these states will facilitate a lasting, balanced, and resilient success, in whatever endeavors you undertake (for example, professional career, creative pursuits, parenting) while also drawing other people close to you. In short, using them will give you not only grit but grace. It will ensure that you'll maximize not only your résumé virtues, to borrow a phrase from David Brooks, but your eulogy ones as well.

ACKNOWLEDGMENTS

It's important to practice what you preach, and in the present case, that couldn't be easier. I have much for which to be grateful, and so I want to take this opportunity to express it. First and foremost, I want to give my most heartfelt and resounding thanks to my wife, Amy, without whom this book never would have come to be. It was through her encouragement that I began the process, and with her sage advice and support that I finished it. Throughout the time that I worked on this book, she wore many hats: idea generator, sounding board, critic, and editor. Without her input, this project would have been much the poorer. I also want to thank my two daughters, who each day show me by example how to embody gratitude and compassion. I'm prouder of them, and more grateful to them, than I can ever express.

I'm grateful to my parents, Vera and Larry DeSteno, for the encouragement and support they've given me over these past forty-nine years. I'm sad to say that I lost my father while I was working on this project, but his passing reminded me all the more of how important it is to build a life that celebrates not only our professional successes but our personal ones — our family ones — as well.

I was raised as an only child, yet I've also been blessed by marriage with a second set of parents and a brother- and sister-in-law who truly make me feel as if I've known them all my life. And so to Joan and Patrick Vitale, Thomas Vitale, Donna Pilato, and their respective families, I extend a hearty thanks for your support and interest in my work. The ideas in this book are all the better for the comments that were traded back and forth across the table at every holiday meal.

I've had the good fortune to run a lab filled with people who are as smart as they are kind and generous. Much of the work described in this book wouldn't have been possible without the ideas and hard work of my present and former graduate students: Monica Bartlett, Leah Dickens, Fred Duong, Daniel Lim, Piercarlo Valdesolo, Lisa Williams, and Jolie Wormwood. Working with each of them has been an honor, and I will forever be grateful to count them not only among my students but among my friends.

It's true, of course, that lots of good science never makes it beyond academic libraries. And so here I would like to extend big thanks to my longtime agent, Jim Levine, and the crew at the Levine, Greenberg, Rostan Literary Agency. As is usually the case, Jim helped me turn a somewhat amorphous set of ideas into a package that resonated with people, and expertly guided consideration of it through the pitching and writing process.

And speaking of pitching and writing, I will forever be grateful to my editor at Houghton Mifflin Harcourt: Eamon Dolan. It was Eamon who believed in the promise of this book, but more important, it was also he who helped polish it. I often talk about the importance of short-term pain for long-term gain. Never did I live it more than as I struggled to respond to Eamon's notes and queries over multiple drafts of the manuscript. Through questioning my assertions, my logic, and my narrative, Eamon helped me to express my ideas in a sharper and more compelling way than I ever could have on my own. I count myself fortunate to have had the opportunity to work with an editor of his caliber.

I would also like to thank the many brilliant people with whom I've had the opportunity to discuss the ideas that make up this book. It's through their input, questioning, and sharing of knowledge that I've experienced many eureka moments: Andrew Zolli, Lisa Feldman Barrett, Robert Frank, Thomas Gilovich, Peter Salovey, Chade Meng-Tan, Arianna Huffington, Adam Grant, Daniel Gilbert, James Ryerson, Anton Andrews, Harald Becker, Arturo Bejar, Trungram Gyaltrul Rinpoche, Jennifer Lerner, and Ye Li.

Finally, conducting scientific research is an expensive enterprise. Were it not for the generous funding that the National Science Foundation, the John Templeton Foundation, and the Mind and Life Institute provided to me and members of my lab, much of the research described throughout this book would not have been possible. I also owe a good deal of thanks to Northeastern University for supporting my research program since it first brought me on board almost twenty years ago. Not a day goes by that I don't consider myself exceedingly lucky to have been given the opportunity to spend my career trying to unlock the secrets of the human mind and hopefully, in so doing, empowering people to live happier, healthier, and more productive lives.

NOTES

Introduction: Self-Control, Success, and the Road Not Taken

PAGE

2 *If anything, our impatience:* For reviews, see Paul Roberts, *The Impulse Society* (New York: Bloomsbury, 2014), as well as "Main Findings: Teens, Technology, and Human Potential in 2020," Pew Research Center, http://www.pewinternet.org/2012/02/29/main -findings-teens-technology-and-human-potential-in-2020/ (accessed April 11, 2017).

3 *On any given day:* Wilhelm Hofmann et al., "Everyday Temptations: An Experience Sampling Study of Desire, Conflict, and Self-Control," *Journal of Personality and Social Psychology* 102 (2012): 1318–35, doi:10.1037/a0026545.

10 *What it did predict:* Angela Duckworth et al., "Grit: Perseverance and Passion for Long-Term Goals," *Journal of Personality and Social Psychology* 92 (2007): 1087–1101, doi:10.1037/0022-3514.92.6.1087.

11 *They found that people:* Christopher Boyce, Alex Wood, and Gordon Brown, "The Dark Side of Conscientiousness: Conscientious People Experience Greater Drops in Life Satisfaction Following Unemployment," *Journal of Research in Personality* 44 (2010): 535–39, doi: 10.1016/j.jrp.2010.05.001.

CHAPTER 1 The Problem: Why and How We All Devalue the Future

18 *They not only had better grades:* Walter Mischel, *The Marshmallow Test: Mastering Self-Control* (New York: Little, Brown, 2014).

24 *The average ADF:* David DeSteno et al., "Gratitude: A Tool for Reducing Economic Impatience," *Psychological Science* 25 (2014): 1262–67, doi:10.1177/0956797614529979.

25 *After having people:* Vladas Griskevicius et al., "When the Economy Falters, Do People Spend or Save? Responses to Resource Scarcity Depend on Childhood Environments," *Psychological Science* 24 (2013): 197–205, doi:10.1177/0956797612451471.
A similar logic: Carol Dweck, *Mindset: The New Psychology of Success* (New York: Ballantine Books, 2007).

29 *Yet when confronted:* David DeSteno and Piercarlo Valdesolo, "The Duality of Virtue: Deconstructing the Moral Hypocrite," *Journal of Experimental Social Psychology* 44 (2008): 1334–38, doi:10.1016/j.jesp.2008.03.010.

30 *90 percent of our participants cheated:* David DeSteno and Piercarlo Valdesolo, "Moral Hypocrisy: Social Groups and the Flexibility of Virtue," *Psychological Science* 18 (2007): 689–90, doi:10.1111/j.1467 -9280.2007.01961.x.

CHAPTER 2 The Problem with the Solution: Why Willpower, Executive Function, and Reason Set You Up for Failure

33 *When the kids focused:* Walter Mischel, Yuichi Shoda, and Monica Rodriguez, "Delay of Gratification in Children," *Science* 244 (1989): 933–38, doi:10.1126/science.2658056.

35   *Decisions reflecting:* Samuel M. McClure et al., "Separate Neural
Systems Value Immediate and Delayed Monetary Rewards," *Science*
306 (2004): 503–507, doi:10.1126/science.1100907.

More than three hundred: Baruch Spinoza, *Theological-Political Treatise,*
eds. S. Shirley and S. Feldman (1670; reprint, Cambridge, MA: Hackett,
2001).

36   *Through the centuries:* See Adam Smith, *The Theory of Moral
Sentiments* (1790; reprint, Oxford: Clarendon Press, 1976), and
Robert Frank, *Passions Within Reason* (New York: W. W. Norton,
1988).

39   *These emotions:* Jennifer Lerner, Ye Li, and Elke Weber, "The
Financial Costs of Sadness," *Psychological Science* 24 (2013): 72–79,
doi:10.1177/0956797612450302, and David DeSteno et al., "Gratitude:
A Tool for Reducing Economic Impatience," *Psychological Science* 25
(2014): 1262–67, doi:10.1177/0956797614529979.

43   *Their answers made clear:* David DeSteno and Piercarlo Valdesolo,
"The Duality of Virtue: Deconstructing the Moral Hypocrite,"
Journal of Experimental Social Psychology 44 (2008): 1334–38,
doi:10.1016/j.jesp.2008.03.010.

After all, in most: Francesca Righetti and Catrin Finkenauer, "If
You Are Able to Control Yourself, I Will Trust You: The Role of
Perceived Self-Control in Interpersonal Trust," *Journal of Personality
and Social Psychology* 100 (2011): 874–76, doi:10.1-37/a0021827.

44   *Greene found that the cheaters:* Joshua Greene and Joseph Paxton,
"Patterns of Neural Activity Associated with Honest and Dishonest
Moral Decisions," *Proceedings of the National Academy of Sciences
of the United States* 106 (2009): 12506–511, doi:De10.1073/
pnas.0900152106.

The kids who were taught: Xiao Pan Ding et al., "Theory-of-Mind
Training Causes Honest Young Children to Lie," *Psychological
Science* 26 (2015): 1812–21, doi:10.1177/0956797615604628.

46   *In fact, as work by:* Sonya Sachdeva, Rumen Iliev, and Douglas
Medin, "Sinning Saints and Saintly Sinners: The Paradox of Moral

Self-Regulation," *Psychological Science* 20 (2009): 523–28, doi:10.1111/j.1467-9280.2009.02326.x.

47 *This isn't because:* Robert Kurzban et al., "An Opportunity Cost Model of Subjective Effort and Task Performance," *Behavioral and Brain Sciences* 36 (2013): 661–79, doi:10.1017/S0140525X12003196. *Many experiments confirm:* Gene Brewer et al., "Examining Depletion Theories Under Conditions of Within-Task Transfer," *Journal of Experimental Psychology: General* 146 (2017): 988–1008, doi:10.1037/xge0000290.

49 *But those who had earlier:* Roy Baumeister et al., "Ego Depletion: Is the Active Self a Limited Resource?" *Journal of Personality and Social Psychology* 74 (1998): 1252–65, doi:10.1037/0022-3514.74.5.1252. *Similar work:* Nicole Mead et al., "Too Tired to Tell the Truth: Self-Control Resource Depletion and Dishonesty," *Journal of Experimental Social Psychology* 45 (2009): 594–97, doi:10.1016/j.jesp.2009.02.004.

50 *Those who regularly:* Wilhelm Hofmann et al., "Everyday Temptations: An Experience Sampling Study of Desire, Conflict, and Self-Control," *Journal of Personality and Social Psychology* 102 (2012): 1318–35, doi:10.1037/a0026545.
Work by Stanford psychologist: Jane Richards and James Gross, "Emotion Regulation and Memory: The Cognitive Costs of Keeping One's Cool," *Journal of Personality and Social Psychology* 79 (2000): 410–24, doi:10.1037/0022-3514.79.3.410.

51 *A team led by:* Gregory Miller et al., "Self-Control Forecasts Better Psychosocial Outcomes but Faster Epigenetic Aging in Low-SES Youth," *Proceedings of the National Academy of Sciences of the United States* 112 (2015): 10325–30, doi:10.1073/pnas.1505063112.

53 *Duckworth and Galla found:* Brian Galla and Angela Duckworth, "More Than Resisting Temptation: Beneficial Habits Mediate the Relationship Between Self-Control and Positive Life Outcomes," *Journal of Personality and Social Psychology* 109 (2015): 508–25, doi:10.1037/pspp0000026.

CHAPTER 3   **Gratitude Is About the Future, Not the Past**

62   *Rather, it was the level:* Monica Bartlett and David DeSteno, "Gratitude and Prosocial Behavior: Helping When It Costs You," *Psychological Science* 17 (2006): 319–25, doi:10.1111/j.1467 -9280.2006.01705.x.

64   *In his well-known analysis:* Adam Grant, *Give and Take: Why Helping Others Drives Our Success* (New York: Viking, 2013).

66   *It took $31:* David DeSteno et al., "Gratitude: A Tool for Reducing Economic Impatience," *Psychological Science* 25 (2014): 1262–67, doi:10.1177/0956797614529979.

67   *To get a sense of how:* Leah Dickens and David DeSteno, "The Grateful Are Patient: Heightened Daily Gratitude Is Associated with Attenuated Temporal Discounting," *Emotion* 16 (2016): 421–25, doi:10.1037/emo0000176.

68   *This observation jibes:* Blair Saunders, Frank He, and Michael Inzlicht, "No Evidence That Gratitude Enhances Neural Performance Monitoring of Conflict-Driven Control," *PLoS ONE* 10 (2015), article e0143312.

69   *Likewise, it's no surprise:* Jeane Twenge and Tim Kasser, "Generational Changes in Materialism and Work Centrality, 1967– 2007: Associations with Temporal Changes in Societal Insecurity and Materialistic Role Modeling," *Personality and Social Psychology Bulletin* 39 (2013): 883–97, doi:10.1177/0146167213485866. *He found exactly:* Jeffrey Froh et al., "Gratitude and the Reduced Costs of Materialism in Adolescents," *Journal of Happiness Studies* 12 (2011): 289–302, doi:10.1007/s10902-010-9195-9.

71   *Doctors who were feeling:* Carlos Estrada, Alice Isen, and Mark Young, "Positive Affect Facilitates Integration of Information and Decreases Anchoring in Reasoning Among Physicians," *Organizational Behavior and Human Decision Processes* 72 (1997): 117–35, doi:10.1006/obhd.1997.2734. *In surveying:* Jesse Walker, Amit Kumar, and Thomas Gilovich,

"Cultivating Gratitude and Giving Through Experiential Consumption," *Emotion* 16 (2016): 1126–36, doi:10.1037/emo0000242.

72 *For example, increased:* Yan-Lei Chen et al., "Relation of Tobacco and Alcohol Use to Stressful Life Events and Gratitude in Middle School Students," *Chinese Mental Health Journal* 26 (2012): 796–800. *Likewise, it helps:* Paul Mills et al., "The Role of Gratitude in Spiritual Well-Being in Asymptomatic Heart Failure Patients," *Spirituality in Clinical Practice* 2 (2015): 5–17, doi:10.1037/scp0000050.

75 *After nine weeks:* Robert Emmons and Michael McCullough, "Counting Blessings Versus Burdens: Experimental Studies of Gratitude and Subjective Well-Being in Daily Life," *Journal of Personality and Social Psychology* 84 (2003): 377–89, doi:10.1037/0022-3514.84.2.377.

76 *One intriguing:* Prathik Kini et al., "The Effects of Gratitude Expression on Neural Activity," *NeuroImage* 128 (2015): 1–10, doi:10.1016/j.neuroimage.2015.12.040.

78 *My friend Robert Frank:* Robert H. Frank, *Success and Luck: Good Fortune and the Myth of Meritocracy* (Princeton, NJ: Princeton University Press, 2016).

CHAPTER 4 Compassion Builds Inner Strength and Inner Peace

82 *The underlying idea:* Hal Hershfield et al., "Increasing Saving Behavior Through Age-Progressed Renderings of the Future Self," *Journal of Marketing Research* 48 (2011): S23–37, doi:10.1509/jmkr.48.SPL.S23.

88 *As it turned out:* Paul Condon et al., "Meditation Increases Compassionate Responses to Suffering," *Psychological Science* 24 (2013): 2125–27, doi:10.1177/0956797613485603.

89 *That's a big difference:* Daniel Lim, Paul Condon, and David DeSteno, "Mindfulness and Compassion: An Examination of Mechanism and Scalability," *PLoS ONE* 10 (2015), doi:10.1371/journal

.pone.0118221, and Helen Weng et al., "Compassion Training Alters Altruism and Neural Responses to Suffering," *Psychological Science* 24 (2013): 1171–80, doi:10.1177/0956797612469537.

93 *While in the moment:* Anna Dreber et al., "Winners Don't Punish," *Nature* 452 (2008): 348–51, doi:10.1038/nature06723.

94 *Although there are many lab-based:* Peter Giancola, "Executive Functioning: A Conceptual Framework for Alcohol-Related Aggression," *Experimental and Clinical Psychopharmacology* 8 (2000): 576–97, doi:10.1037/1064-1297.8.4.576.

95 *When the floodgates opened:* Eli Finkel et al., "Using I³ Theory to Clarify When Dispositional Aggressiveness Predicts Intimate Partner Violence Perpetration," *Journal of Personality and Social Psychology* 102 (2012): 533–49, doi:10.1037/a0025651.

96 *As they anticipated, the simple:* Francesca Gino, Shahar Ayal, and Dan Ariely, "Contagion and Differentiation in Unethical Behavior: The Effect of One Bad Apple on the Barrel," *Psychological Science* 20 (2009): 393–98, doi:10.1111/j.1467-9280.2009.02306.x.

98 *But when they poured:* Condon et al., "Meditation Increases Compassionate Responses."

99 *Simply put, their aggression:* Ibid.

    Work by Harvard's Martin: Dreber et al., "Winners Don't Punish."

103 *The students who were encouraged:* Juliana Breines and Serena Chen, "Self-Compassion Increases Self-Improvement Motivation," *Personality and Social Psychology Bulletin* 38 (2012): 1133–43, doi:10.1177/0146167212445599.B.

    Students who typically: Alison Flett, Mohsen Haghbin, and Timothy Pychyl, "Procrastination and Depression from a Cognitive Perspective: An Exploration of the Associations Among Procrastinatory Automatic Thoughts, Rumination, and Mindfulness," *Journal of Rational-Emotive and Cognitive-Behavior Therapy* 34 (2016): 169–86, doi:10.1007/s10942-016-0235-1.

    Those who more regularly: Leah Ferguson et al., "Exploring Self-Compassion and Eudaimonic Well-Being in Young Women

Athletes," *Journal of Sport and Exercise Psychology* 36 (2014): 203–16, doi:10.1123/jsep.2013-0096.

A similar pattern: Cathy Magnus, Kent Kowalski, and Tara-Leigh McHugh, "The Role of Self-Compassion in Women's Self-Determined Motives to Exercise and Exercise-Related Outcomes," *Self and Identity* 9 (2010): 363–82, doi:10.1080/15298860903135073.

For example, smokers: Allison Kelly et al., "Who Benefits from Training in Self-Compassionate Self-Regulation? A Study of Smoking Reduction," *Journal of Social and Clinical Psychology* 29 (2010): 727–55, doi:10.1521/jscp.2010.29.7.727.

104 *All of these are controlled:* Stephen Porges, "Vagal Tone: A Physiologic Marker of Stress Vulnerability," *Pediatrics* 90 (1992): 498–504.

When she induced: Jennifer Stellar et al., "Affective and Physiological Responses to the Suffering of Others: Compassion and Vagal Activity," *Journal of Personality and Social Psychology* 108 (2015): 572–85, doi:10.1037/pspi0000010.

105 *When she subjected:* Karen Bluth et al., "Does Self-Compassion Protect Adolescents from Stress?" *Journal of Child and Family Studies* 25 (2016): 1098–1109, doi:10.1007/s10826-015-0307-3.

106 *Once again, those who:* Lim, Condon, and DeSteno, "Mindfulness and Compassion."

109 *Nonetheless, that increased:* Piercarlo Valdesolo and David DeSteno, "Synchrony and the Social Tuning of Compassion," *Emotion* 11 (2011): 262–66, doi:10.1037/a0021302.

CHAPTER 5 **Pride and Perseverance**

118 *Chimps, like humans:* Alicia P. Melis, Brian Hare, and Michael Tomasello, "Engineering Cooperation in Chimpanzees: Tolerance Constraints on Cooperation," *Animal Behavior* 72 (2006): 275–86, and "Chimpanzees Recruit the Best Collaborators," *Science* 311 (March 3, 2006): 1297–1300.

So it should come: Jessica Tracy, Azim Shariff, and Joey Cheng,

"A Naturalist's View of Pride," *Emotion Review* 2 (2010): 163–77, doi:10.1177/1754073909354627.

123 *Beginning in the 1970s:* Albert Bandura, "Self-Efficacy: Toward a Unifying Theory of Behavioral Change," *Psychological Review* 84 (1977): 191–215, doi:10.1037/0033-295X.84.2.191.

They upped the time: Lisa Williams and David DeSteno, "Pride and Perseverance: The Motivational Role of Pride," *Journal of Personality and Social Psychology* 94 (2008): 1007–17, doi:10.1037/0022-3514.94 .6.1007.

Those who believed: When we asked people how well they believed they performed compared with their peers, participants in both the self-efficacy and the pride conditions reported elevated expectations. Of import, both groups believed they had performed equally well, thereby ruling out the possibility that the increased perseverance among those feeling pride might be due to even greater feelings of self-efficacy.

124 *While those feeling pride:* Williams and DeSteno, "Pride and Perseverance."

For example, feeling pride: Willem Verbeke, Frank Belschak, and Richard Bagozzi, "The Adaptive Consequences of Pride in Personal Selling," *Journal of the Academy of Marketing Science* 32 (2004): 386–402, doi:10.1177/0092070304267105.

In a similar vein: Aaron Weidman, Jessica Tracy, and Andrew Elliot, "The Benefits of Following Your Pride: Authentic Pride Promotes Achievement," *Journal of Personality* 84 (2016): 607–22, doi:10.1111/ jopy.121.

125 *The instances in which people:* Wilhelm Hofmann and Rachel Fisher, "How Guilt and Pride Shape Subsequent Self-Control," *Social Psychological and Personality Science* 3 (2012): 682–90, doi:10.1177/1948550611435136.

Using an economic: Shi-Yun Ho, Eddie Tong, and Lile Jia, "Authentic and Hubristic Pride: Differential Effects on Delay of Gratification," *Emotion* 16 (2016): 1147–56, doi:10.1037/emo0000179.

126 *Those who are viewed:* Francesca Righetti and Catrin Finkenauer,

"If You Are Able to Control Yourself, I Will Trust You: The Role of Perceived Self-Control in Interpersonal Trust," *Journal of Personality and Social Psychology* 100 (2011): 874–76, doi:10.1-37/a0021827.

Time and again her research: Tracy, Shariff, and Cheng, "Naturalist's View of Pride."

127 *When we asked our:* Lisa Williams and David DeSteno, "Pride: Adaptive Social Emotion or Seventh Sin?" *Psychological Science* 20 (2009): 284–88, doi:10.1111/j.1467-9280.2009.02292.x.

130 *On the days where:* Mark Lepper, David Greene, and Richard Nisbett, "Undermining Children's Intrinsic Interest with Extrinsic Reward: A Test of the Overjustification Hypothesis," *Journal of Personality and Social Psychology* 28 (1973): 129–37, doi:10.1037/h0035519.

Even when material: Edward Deci, Richard Koestner, and Richard Ryan, "A Meta-Analytic Review of Experiments Examining the Effects of Extrinsic Rewards," *Psychological Bulletin* 125 (1999): 627–68, doi:10.1037/0033-2909.125.6.627.

132 *Abundant research shows:* Richard Ryan and Edward Deci, "Self-Determination Theory and the Facilitation of Intrinsic Motivation, Social Development, and Well-Being," *American Psychologist* 55 (2000): 68–78, doi:10.1037/0003-066X.55.1.68.

Children whose parents: Christina Frederick and Richard Ryan, "Self-Determination in Sport: A Review Using Cognitive Evaluation Theory," *International Journal of Sport Psychology* 26 (1995): 5–23.

133 *Likewise, feelings of social:* Gregory Walton and Geoffrey Cohen, "A Brief Social-Belonging Intervention Improves Academic and Health Outcomes of Minority Students," *Science* 331 (2011): 1447–51, doi:10.1126/science.1198364.

135 *Put another way:* Edward Thorndike coined the term "halo effect" and demonstrated its earliest scientific documentation. Specifically, Thorndike showed that superiors' performance evaluations of their subordinates' traits and abilities evidence implausible correlations. For example, most people were judged to be either uniformly good or uniformly bad.

136 *Likewise, most adults:* David Landy and Harold Sigall, "Beauty Is

Talent: Task Evaluation as a Function of the Performer's Physical Attractiveness," *Journal of Personality and Social Psychology* 29 (1974): 299–304, doi:10.1037/h0036018.

In studying a thousand people: Charles Carver, Sungchoon Sinclair, and Sheri Johnson, "Authentic and Hubristic Pride: Differential Relations to Aspects of Goal Regulation, Affect, and Self-Control," *Journal of Research in Personality* 44 (2010): 698–703, doi:10.1016/j.jrp.2010.09.004.

137 *Whereas hubristic:* Tracy, Shariff, and Cheng, "Naturalist's View of Pride."

138 *A full 40 percent:* Vanessa Patrick, HaeEun Helen Chun, and Deborah Macinnis, "Affective Forecasting and Self-Control: Why Anticipating Pride Wins Over Anticipating Shame in a Self-Regulation Context," *Journal of Consumer Psychology* 19 (2009): 537–45, doi:10.1016/j.jcps.2009.05.006.

CHAPTER 6 Being Social Means Being Successful

146 *Not an easy:* Robert Axelrod, *The Evolution of Cooperation* (New York: Basic Books, 1984).

147 *There would be way:* To see why a society characterized by total cooperation or cheating would be unstable, imagine a place where everyone was honest and helpful, where you never had to even consider the possibility that someone would cheat. What would happen? People would trust reflexively. There wouldn't be a need to consider character. Now imagine a person enters this community who, due to some sort of genetic mutation, is willing to cheat and loaf. His resources would skyrocket, as he would take everyone for a sucker. Because of his success, he'd produce more progeny in the next generation — a pattern that would continue until everyone began to stop trusting reflexively and adopted cheating ways due to the benefits offered. But once cheating became the dominant strategy, the few who would decide to cooperate would begin to accrue greater gains and preferentially seek out others with the self-control to be virtuous.

And so, the cooperators would rise. The result, as Martin Nowak, Robert Frank, and others have shown, would be a fluctuating equilibrium of cooperators and cheaters.

So while simulations: Martin Nowak and Roger Highfield, *Supercooperators* (New York: Free Press, 2011).

149 *Framing the rewards:* Gregory Walton et al., "Mere Belonging: The Power of Social Connections," *Journal of Personality and Social Psychology* 102 (2012): 513–32, doi:10.1037/a0025731. It should also be noted that the perseverance and motivation of those who had read the skills-based article didn't differ from that of students who hadn't read any article. Thus, emphasizing individualized skills did not reduce motivation from what it would normally be but rather emphasizing the social aspects increased motivation.

150 *The sense of being:* Ibid.

151 *As the researchers expected:* Tara Dennehy and Nilanjana Dasgupta, "Female Peer Mentors Early in College Increase Women's Positive Academic Experiences and Retention in Engineering," *Proceedings of the National Academy of Sciences of the United States* 114 (2017): 5964–69, doi:10.1073/pnas.1613117114.

153 *The findings were impressive:* Gregory Walton and Geoffrey Cohen, "A Brief Social-Belonging Intervention Improves Academic and Health Outcomes of Minority Students," *Science* 331 (2011): 1447–51, doi:10.1126/science.1198364.

155 *Attendance at club:* Robert Putnam, *Bowling Alone: The Collapse and Revival of American Community* (New York: Simon and Schuster, 2000).

The result is that: "The Lonely States of America," CBS News, http://www.cbsnews.com/news/the-lonely-states-of-america/ (accessed April 17, 2017).

156 *Those who were excluded:* Naomi Eisenberger, Matthew Lieberman, and Kipling Williams, "Does Rejection Hurt? An fMRI Study of Social Exclusion," *Science* 302 (2003): 290–92, doi:10.1126/science.1089134.

Over time, the chronic: "AAAS 2014: Loneliness Is a Major Health

Risk for Older Adults," University of Chicago News, https://news. uchicago.edu/article/2014/02/16/aaas-2014-loneliness-major-health-risk-older-adults (accessed April 17, 2017).

The experience of that: Lydialyle Gibson, "The Nature of Loneliness," *University of Chicago Magazine,* http://magazine.uchicago.edu/1012 /features/the-nature-of-loneliness.shtml (accessed April 17, 2017).

157   *And this "transmission":* John Cacioppo, James Fowler, and Nicholas Christakis, "Alone in the Crowd: The Structure and Spread of Loneliness in a Large Social Network," *Journal of Personality and Social Psychology* 97 (2009): 977–91, doi:10.1037/a0016076.

158   *In reviewing survey data:* Emily Bianchi and Kathleen Vohs, "Social Class and Social Worlds: Income Predicts the Frequency and Nature of Social Contact," *Social Psychological and Personality Science* 7 (2016): 479–86, doi:10.1177/1948550616641472.

159   *Two examples:* John Cacioppo and Louise Hawkley, "Perceived Social Isolation and Cognition," *Trends in Cognitive Science* 13 (2009): 447–54, doi:10.1016/j.tics.2009.06.005.

Those who were lonely: Hakan Ozcelik and Sigal Barsade, "Work Loneliness and Employee Performance," *Academy of Management Proceedings,* January 2011 Meeting Abstract Supplement): 1–6, doi:10.5465/ambpp.2011.65869714.

CHAPTER 7   Scaling Out: Reaching High Means Reaching Out

162   *When colleges and recruitment:* "Well-Rounded Versus Angular: The Application Colleges Want to See," WBUR News. http://legacy. wbur.org/2013/12/26/well-rounded-passion-college-application (accessed May 15, 2017).

164   *Fair or not:* And, unfortunately, playing "catch up" isn't always an option. As we saw in chapter 3, when students from disadvantaged backgrounds tried to employ executive function strategies to help them achieve in college, it came at a cost. These students didn't have the luxury of having doors opened for them early on, and when they were trying to use cognitive self-control skills to master their academics, their health suffered.

166 *Those who worked in units:* Sigal Barsade and Olivia O'Neill, "What's Love Got to Do with It? A Longitudinal Study of the Culture of Companionate Love and Employee and Client Outcomes in a Long-Term Care Setting," *Administrative Science Quarterly* 59 (2014): 551–98, doi:10.1177/0001839214538636.

167 *At the end of the program:* Christine Yeh et al., "Fostering Social Support, Leadership Competence, Community Engagement, and Resilience Among Samoan American Youth," *Asian American Journal of Psychology* 6 (2015): 145–53, doi:10.1037/a0038545.

168 *So depending:* Daniel Kahneman and Angus Deaton, "High Income Improves Evaluation of Life but Not Emotional Well-Being," *Proceedings of the National Academy of Sciences of the United States* 107 (2010): 16489–93, doi:10.1073/pnas.1011492107.

169 *People who spent:* Elizabeth Dunn, Lara Aknin, and Michael Norton, "Spending Money on Others Promotes Happiness," *Science* 319 (2008): 1687–88, doi:10.1126/science.1150952.

170 *Giving of any kind:* William Harbaugh, Ulrich Mayr, and Daniel Burghart, "Neural Responses to Taxation and Voluntary Giving Reveal Motives for Charitable Donations," *Science* 316 (2007): 1622–25, doi:10.1126/science.1140738.
    What psychologists call: Eva Telzer et al., "Neural Sensitivity to Eudaimonic and Hedonic Rewards Differentially Predict Adolescent Depressive Symptoms Over Time," *Proceedings of the National Academy of Sciences of the United States* 111 (2014): 6600–6605, doi:10.1073/pnas.1323014111.

171 *All emotions are:* Elaine Hatfield, John Cacioppo, and Richard Rapson, "Emotional Contagion," *Current Directions in Psychological Science* 2 (1993): 96–99, doi:10.1111/1467-8721.ep10770953.

172 *The results were unambiguous:* Adam Kramer, Jamie Guillory, and Jeffrey Hancock, "Experimental Evidence of Massive-Scale Emotional Contagion Through Social Networks," *Proceedings of the National Academy of Sciences of the United States* 111 (2014): 8788–90, doi:10.1073/pnas.1320040111.

173 *In the realm of cooperation:* Alexander Peysakhovich and David Rand,

"Habits of Virtue: Creating Norms of Cooperation and Defection in the Laboratory," *Management Science* 62 (2016): 631–47, doi:10.1287/mnsc.2015.2168.

175 *Whereas the average:* Adam Grant and Francesca Gino, "A Little Thanks Goes a Long Way: Explaining Why Gratitude Expressions Motivate Prosocial Behavior," *Journal of Personality and Social Psychology* 98 (2010): 946–55, doi:10.1037/a0017935.

Specifically, they showed: Adam Grant and Amy Wrzesniewski, "I Won't Let You Down . . . or Will I? Core Self-Evaluations, Other-Orientation, Anticipated Guilt and Gratitude, and Job Performance," *Journal of Applied Psychology* 95 (2010): 108–21, doi:10.1037/a0017974.

CHAPTER 8 Scaling Up: Stimulating Societal Success

180 *And so, for many:* Even though cooperation drops, remember that there are some people who remain generous. It is these individuals who, over time, will find others who are also generous and thus begin to experience the benefits of cooperation. For this reason, generosity will never be completely extinguished; rather it will ebb and flow as a function of group norms for giving.

A poll from 2015: "Most Republicans Say They Back Climate Action, Poll Finds," *New York Times,* January 30, 2015, https://www.nytimes.com/2015/01/31/us/politics/most-americans-support-government-action-on-climate-change-poll-finds.html?version=meter+at+0&module=meter-Links&pgtype=article&contentId=&mediaId=&referrer=&priority=true&action=click&contentCollection=meter-links-click (accessed April 17, 2017).

This widely distributed: Geoffrey Heal, "Discounting and Climate Change: An Editorial Comment," *Climatic Change* 37 (1997): 335–43, doi:10.1023/a:1005384629724. https://www.researchgate.net/profile/Geoffrey_Heal2/publication/226289791_Discounting_and_Climate_Change_An_Editorial_Comment/links/02bfe51155c6a82b2e000000.pdf.

181 *In fact, in 2010:* "Building the Bridges to a Sustainable Recovery," *New*

York Times, September 11, 2010, http://www.nytimes.com/2010 /09/12/business/economy/12view.html?mwrsm=Email&_r=1 (accessed April 17, 2017).

Cornell economist Robert: Ibid.

184 *The focus on purity:* Jesse Graham, Jonathan Haidt, and Brian Nosek, "Liberals and Conservatives Rely on Different Sets of Moral Foundations," *Journal of Personality and Social Psychology* 96 (2009): 1029–46, doi:10.1037/a0015141.

The conservatives who'd: Matthew Feinberg and Robb Willer, "The Moral Roots of Environmental Attitudes," *Psychological Science* 24 (2013): 56–62, doi:10.1177/0956797612449177.

187 *The results were impressive:* Erez Yoeli et al., "Powering Up with Indirect Reciprocity in a Large-Scale Field Experiment," *Proceedings of the National Academy of Sciences of the United States* 110 (2013): 10424–29, doi:10.1073/pnas.1301210110.

188 *And it's a view backed:* Damon Jones, Mark Greenberg, and Max Crowley, "Early Social-Emotional Functioning and Public Health: The Relationship Between Kindergarten Social Competence and Future Wellness," *American Journal of Public Health* 105 (2015): 2283–90, doi:10.2105/ajph.2015.302630.

190 *No, their minds were:* Erin Hennes et al., "Motivated Recall in the Service of the Economic System: The Case of Anthropogenic Climate Change," *Journal of Experimental Psychology: General* 145 (2016): 755–71, doi:10.1037/xge0000148.

Coda

194 *As* New York Times *reporter:* "Why What You Learned in Preschool Is Crucial at Work," *New York Times,* October 18, 2015, www.nytimes .com/2015/10/18/upshot/how-the-modern-workplace-has-become -more-like-preschool.html (accessed April 17, 2017).

Other jobs: David Deming, "The Growing Importance of Social Skills in the Labor Market," *National Bureau of Economic Research,* NBER Working Paper No. 21473 (2015).

195 *While many Google employees:* Adam Bryant, "Google's Quest to Build a Better Boss," *New York Times,* March 13, 2011, www.nytimes .com/2011/03/13/business/13hire.html (accessed April 17, 2017).

196 *And as Harvard's Teresa:* Teresa Amabile, Constance Hadley, and Steven Kramer, "Creativity Under the Gun," *Harvard Business Review,* August 2002, https://hbr.org/2002/08/creativity-under-the -gun (accessed May 18, 2017).

198 *In a series of experiments:* Gale Lucas et al., "When the Going Gets Tough: Grit Predicts Costly Perseverance," *Journal of Research in Personality* 59 (2015): 15–22, doi:10.1016/j.jrp.2015.08.004.

INDEX